I0408083

THE HAPPINESS
User's manual for humans

RICARDO LAMPUGNANI

Cover Art and inside design: ©Aneley Lampugnani
Translation by: Aneley Lampugnani and Louise Warr
Language revision by: Louise Warr
Edited by: ©Àrbora books 2017

CONTENT

The Happiness.
User's manual for humans

<< A SEEKER IS SOMEONE WHO LOOKS FOR SOMETHING, BUT NOT NECESSARILY SOMEONE WHO FINDS IT. NOR IS SOMEONE WHO NECESSARILY KNOWS WHAT HE IS LOOKING FOR, IS SIMPLY SOMEONE FOR WHOM LIFE IS A QUEST>>

JORGE BUCAY

The Happiness.
User's manual for humans

INTRODUCTION

For many years, I have asked myself how it is possible that human beings are not born with an instructions manual. It would have been very useful for me; to understand my own nature and to avoid making mistakes so many times in my life. I especially missed having one when my two daughters were born, and very often as they were growing up. But since such manual does not exist, I had to make do with self-help books, metaphysics books and other unofficial types of science. In the beginning, they all seem to show the discovery of the panacea, but after a short time, one gets tired of visualizing, meditating, controlling… and concludes that one is too stupid to follow a path that others walked before to become happy or satisfied with their lives.

Today, after more than half a century of occupying this body of mine, and at the point of entering `the final stage', I have decided to put it all down in a Word archive, everything I have learnt after investigating, searching for solutions to my problems, and explanations to the situations I have been through. And they are not few.

At this point, one could think: *"So WHAT? WE ARE ALL DIFFERENT, WE HAVE DIFFERENT LIFE EXPERIENCES AND THEY ARE UNIQUE"*

That is true. However, my experience in the field of industrial engineering has taught me to solve complicated situations by unravelling their intricacies to reveal the simple problems of which they are made.

Let us —then, simplify this explanation: if we have a tangled skein of yarn and we try to untangle it all at the same time, we will surely not be able to do so. Instead, if we take one thread at the time, we will most likely succeed.

The human being is a skein of yarn which is both very complex and very tangled, even for scientists themselves. Or maybe precisely because they are scientists and they must prove everything they claim; they find themselves more often uncertain than certain of how the human being works.

I am not a scientist; I'm not trying to prove anything or reinvent the wheel. I only want to describe the view I have from where I find myself.

And where do I find myself?

This question is here just so nobody thinks I feel superior or that I believe that I have all the answers to all the questions.

I remember my university years (and I guess the same still happens), we would crowd around the classroom door every time a student came out of an oral exam. We would ask if it had been easy, which subjects they had spoken about, if the examiners were in a good mood... All this questioning didn't help abit, their exam wasn't ours, but it calmed us down. That student had done what we were about to do in a few minutes and that fact granted him *experience*.

This is the point where I find myself. I have gathered experiences along the road, I have looked for answers, I have seen signs, I have tripped and got up again. If this smoothies the path for anyone, I consider myself satisfied. For sure your path will be different from mine, and I cannot walk it for you, but they are all paths. What they have in common is no one knows where they go, until we walk them. Another point we have in common is that:

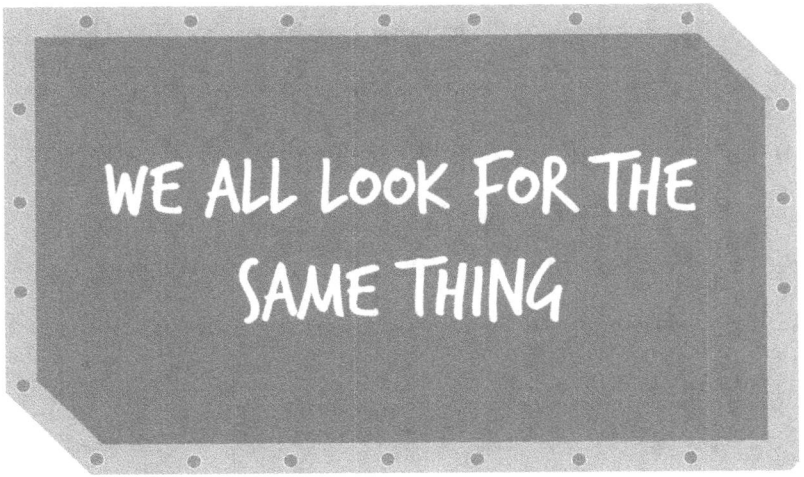

WE ALL LOOK FOR THE SAME THING

Yes; even though you could say that an African, a European or a Chinese or Finnish person, women and men, have nothing in common:

Think again, the common point in all human beings is that...

We spend years and years, from when we are born until we die. In many cases, we wander through our existence as Teseo in the Cretan labyrinth, when he wanted to kill the Minotaur. We walk in circles, leaving our thread of experience behind, and when we pick it up, we can find the exit. There may be more than just one exit, but this is the one I know.

Going back to happiness: I am sure you have heard some of the following phrases.

"Happy he who learns to bear what he cannot change." -Friedrich Schiller.

"I, not events, have the power to make me happy or unhappy today. I can choose which it shall be. Yesterday is dead, tomorrow hasn't arrived yet. I have just one day, today, and I'm going to be happy in it."-Groucho Marx

"Money has never made man happy, nor will it, there is nothing in its nature to produce happiness. The more of it one has the more one wants." -Benjamin Franklin.

"Happiness is not doing what you want to do; it's to love what you do." -Jean Paul Sartre.

"Happiness cannot be found in possessions, or in gold; happiness is in the soul" -Demócrito.

"Happy is the man who has broken the chains which hurt the mind, and has given up worrying once and for all." -Ovidio.

"Happiness doesn't depend on any external conditions, it is governed by our mental attitude." -Dale Carnegie.

"Happiness is not something that is already made. It comes with your own actions." -Dalai Lama.

"Happiness is dependent on self-discipline. We are the biggest obstacles to our own happiness. It is much easier to do battle with society and with others than to fight our own nature."-Dennis Prager.

"The happiness of most people we know is not ruined by great catastrophes or fatal errors, but by the repetition of slowly destructive little things." -Ernest Dimmest.

"The search for happiness is one of the biggest sources of unhappiness." -Eric Hoffer.

"Success is not the key of happiness. Happiness is the key of success. If you love what you do, you will be successful." -Albert Schweitzer.

"Nobody can be happy without self-love." -Jean-Jacques Rousseau.

"To be without some of the things you want is an indispensable part of happiness." -Bertrand Russell.

"Happiness is a how, not a what. It's a talent, not an object." -Herman Hesse.

...I have just copied a few here; there are thousands of quotes on happiness, and I suspect they often contradict each other.

What seems obvious is that the thing we chase all our lives depends more on ourselves than on what happens to us. If this is true, my friend, we are damned, because we hardly know ourselves well enough, and, hence, we do not know how we work. And this is similar to trying to drive a car without knowing the difference between clutch and brakes: we are bound to hit everything that's put in front of us.

When you finish reading this book, if you do decide to finish it, you will not have a recipe for happiness. I can tell you with certainty that such a recipe does not exist. But what I can assure you is that you will probably know a little more about yourself, and about the tools you have at hand to build a happiness that is tailor-made, just for you.

The Happiness.

User's manual for humans

PURPOSE OF THE PRODUCT

The product "human being" has one purpose: being happy. And this simple phrase contains the complexity of existence itself. Taking the core of some of the phrases in the introduction about happiness, the purpose of being happy should be:

1. **TO BE ABLE TO ENDURE WHAT WE CANNOT CHANGE** And I guess that endure means to resist or accept, not resign.

2. **TO TRY AND REACH THE GOAL, TODAY** Do not focus on promises in the future, nor memories from the past.

3. **TO AVOID LOOKING FOR HAPPINESS AS A GOAL**, because the result is the opposite.

4. **TO ACHIEVE THE GOAL OF HAPPINESS**, without stealing anyone else's.

5. **THE GOAL OF THE PRODUCT HUMAN BEING** is not achieved through money.

6. **HAPPINESS CANNOT BE ACHIEVED** doing whatever we want to do.

7. **THE GOAL OF BEING HAPPY IS IN A PLACE** we barely know: our soul.

8. **TO REACH THE PURPOSE OF THE PRODUCT WE NEED TO AVOID WORRYING**, live without some of the things we want to possess, and to break the chains that we carry in our mind.

9. **TO REACH THE GOAL OF THE PRODUCT, WE SHOULD ALSO:** love ourselves, love what we do, and avoid the repetition of small self-destructive actions.

I am guessing that anyone who buys a product with such a complex purpose, feels like sending it back straight away. The problem is that you cannot; or put in another way, the only way of getting rid of it is by destroying it. And this is complicated, because human beings, like all beings, come equipped with a security system called survival instinct.

Consider then, dear User, how we can manage to achieve the objective of this complex product – to make ourselves happy. Sometimes it seems almost impossible. Maybe in an ideal world, being happy would be easier to achieve, but we do not live in such a world.

Branches of marketing and advertising strategies have been created offering products guaranteed to make us happy. Further still the majority of religions offer the faithful eternal happiness when we die, in exchange for certain behaviour in life. But the thing is, nobody has ever come back from Heaven to complain that the promise of happiness was not true.

Nevertheless, my experience tells me that the product human being is equipped with all the tools it needs to achieve happiness, whatever its geographical location and its space-time situation.

THE ONLY THING WE NEED TO LEARN ABOUT ARE ITS COMPONENTS AND HOW THEY WORK.

The Happiness.
User's manual for humans

DESCRIPTION OF THE PRODUCT

The product *human being* has two types of components:

Visible components.

Invisible components.

This may seem like pointing out the obvious. But we need to start somewhere, untangling the skein.

All the different versions of this product we call human being have these components: you can be black, white, yellow, or anything in between. But you do have them, without exception. The same goes for the different types of human beings, male or female with all their characteristic variations, tall, short, thin, fat, heterosexual, homosexual the list is endless… but they all have visible and invisible components.

To summarize, this product -the human being- has happiness as its main objective, and it comes from the factory with visible and invisible components.

The Happiness.

User's manual for humans

VISIBLE COMPONENTS

The visible components consist of the outer case of the product, its control panel, ventilation system, engine, detection sensors, transference mechanism and drainage system. Its functioning is completely automatic and synchronized. It does not need added lubrication and it runs on water and organic matter.

This wonder of engineering is also self-regulating. This means that, any faults occurring during or post fabrication causing breakdown or malfunctions will be over-ridden by other sensors.

The sensor systems are composed of:

❧ **A TWO-DIMENSIONAL VIDEO CAMERA WITH A RESOLUTION OF 576 MEGAPIXELS**[1] which allows differentiation of objects at short and long distances. This camera has an automatic shutter, wide angle of 120 degrees on each side, and 60 degrees vertically.

---

[1] The most powerful camera is the Dark Energy Camera, on top of the Observatory of Cerro Tololo in Chile, and it counts with 570 megapixels through five precision lenses

❗ **A SOUND ANALYSER** which allows detection of frequency and rhythm, and electrochemical transmission of these to the central computer.

❗ **A SCENT CHEMORECEPTOR** which allows distinction between more than 10.000 different aromas.

❗ **A TASTE CHEMORECEPTOR** able to detect five different types of taste: acidic, sweet, sour, salty and umami. It also has a set of tactile sensors which allow us to perceive texture, size and temperature. This system might seem primitive if compared with the rest, but as it is connected to the smell receptor, it can distinguish between an enormous range of taste combinations.

❗ **A TACTILE SYSTEM** which instantaneously activates on contact with another body and perceives the pressure it receives and its temperature. It features more than four million sensors, which are distributed all over the outer casing.

The product human being comes from the factory with a sophisticated security system and alarms against possible external or internal attacks. Likewise, it has the capability of updating its files when attacked by new threats, consequently developing new and effective defences all the time.

Its internal structure, light and resistant has the capability of repairing itself in the case of breakage. Self-lubricated articulations allow for an infinite variety of precise movements. Added to this, a variable running speed of up to 60 km/hour can be achieved in the sportiest models[2].The upper limbs can achieve astonishing precision and speed through repetitive practice. All models come complete with a porous, flexible and durable outer cover. This cover is photosensitive, and it has the ability to darken after sun exposure, as well as becoming lighter in the absence of the sun. The effect is most evident in light-colored models. In addition, it has a device that detects the thermal differences and reacts by sending the information to the rest of the system. The application of any object on its surface is enough to sense the temperature. There is also an efficient equipment for the regulation of humidity and temperature by evaporation of water. Finally, the product human being features a latest generation central computer equipped with three types of memory:

Short term

Long term, and sensory.

---

[2] Usain Bolt, the Olympic Model, can run reach 64 km/h.

The use of dynamic memories allows storage of 2.5 petabytes, that is, approximately one million gigabytes. This equates to about three million hours of video or 300 years of continuous playback.

This ultra mega computer is linked to all the sensor systems and motors from which it receives information and to those who give orders and solve problems.

As you can see, dear User, the product human being is a technological marvel of the latest generation. However, despite its advances, it shares many of its characteristics with other products considered of inferior quality, called *animals*. In fact, there are animals whose visible components exceed those of the human being. Not in everything, but they surpass it in terms of sensory, and safety systems, outer cover durability, speed, flexibility and even precision.

Does that mean that the animal product is preferable to the human being? Or ... Is the product human, part of a broader range generically called *animal*?

THE ANSWER TO THE FIRST QUESTION IS NO. THE ANSWER TO THE SECOND, IS MAYBE.

Although everything indicates that the human being is an animal that has evolved from the primates, the complex equipment that it shares with them is enough to become something special in the universe. The simple fact that millions of atoms have united in a certain way, to offer such sophisticated features, is a miracle.

Therefore, if you have purchased one of these models, you can be satisfied. It will be difficult for you to exhaust its capabilities even if you specifically try.

However, we have spoken only of its visible components, in a brief way. Let's hope you know some of its invisible components.

The Happiness.

User's manual for humans

INVISIBLE COMPONENTS

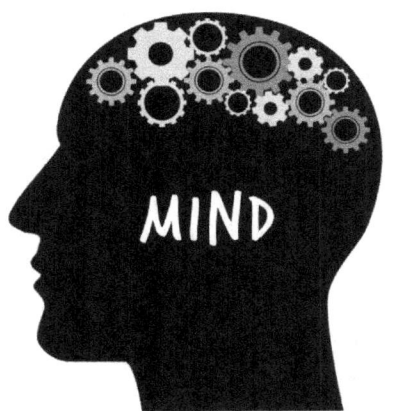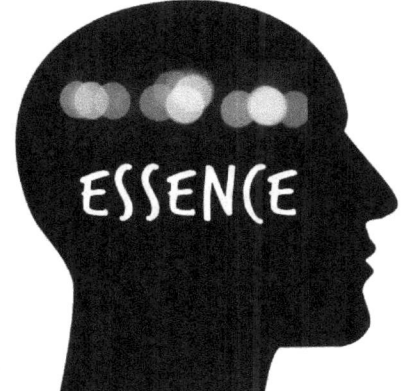

And you could ask: only those two, and with such worn out names that have been used for everything?

YES, FOR SURE. I could have renamed them, but these are widely used terms, even among neuroscientific professionals. To be honest, I could change **ESSENCE** for **SOUL**, but that might be worse.

MIND

The ancient Greeks called the Mind *psyche* or *psyche* although they gave it the meaning of soul and established it at the place where the consciousness or unconsciousness of the product human being resides. Nowadays, the processes attributed to the Mind are:

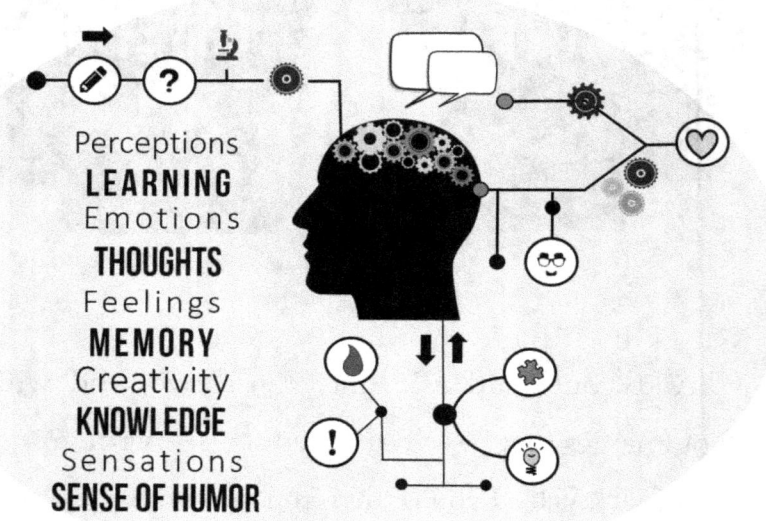

The level of consciousness seems to be a border line over which Mind or Essence, may have control. More details can be found in the section Operating System. In the mind also resides an element called EGO, to which all kinds of qualities have been attributed throughout history, and not always good ones.

Actually, in my experience, I've found there is nothing wrong with the Ego or I, he is just the head of Public relations of the mind. As you can see, the human being product is not only exceptional for its visible components, but also its invisible ones.

The mind doesn't only learn and retain new information; all the data that is entered is corroborated and imbricated with previous knowledge, resulting in a continuously improved and enriched data bank. And the best part is that none of the information that enters the mind can be erased.

WHAT?

You read right: Knowledge cannot be deleted from our minds. Even though, sometimes it seems we have forgotten things, it is enough to activate the memory trigger to retrieve that information as if we have just learnt. Obviously, we are talking about mentally healthy individuals.

Allow me to diverse from the user manual to set a personal example:

A few days ago, I was walking through the city of Tarragona and saw a tree that I knew. It is not indigenous to the Mediterranean, it originates in tropical and subtropical areas of America, so you don't see many here. Despite being familiar, I couldn't remember the scientific name of the tree.

When I saw the leaves, their shape bought back the common name, which is cow's hoof.

Then, like a shot, the scientific name of the tree came to mind (it was a bahuinia candicans).

I also remembered that they call it false mahogany and that its wood is used in cabinet making.

It is true that I used to work with ornamental plants, but that was almost twenty years ago.

Now, as I write the previous anecdote, memories of the past in another country are evoked and, I find myself lying on my back. To the left there is a window that has the blind ajar. Light pours through the cracks making the specks of dust dance in the beams, amusing me. Outside, I can hear the sound of a sweeping broom and a bucket of water that someone empties on the floor. A sense of calm possesses me. I am not alone. My mother washes the yard ... That's what she was doing, fifty-something years ago.

As you can see, the mind does not only store knowledge; it also remembers sensations, emotions, and memories.

HUMAN BEING: WHAT AN INCREDIBLE PRODUCT!

Specialist neurologists around the globe investigate the origins of our sense of humour. It turns out that this capability has no logic explanation. The brain receives a piece of information, processes it and then, for some reason, sends orders to the muscles to contract. It's one of our mind's capabilities; to imagine certain situations we find funny and laugh at them. But not all of these potentially funny situations make us laugh. Some jokes make some people laugh, but have no effect on other people.

As you can see, dear User, thanks to the camera we have incorporated within us we can see, but it is thanks to the capabilities of our mind that we can laugh at a funny story, or perceive beauty in a sunset.

Through our sound analyser, we can listen, but it is thanks to our mind that we actually enjoy music.

A chemoreceptor allows us to smell something, but it is the mind which allows us to decide whether what we smell is a delicious perfume or a disgusting stink. Other receptors help us determine if the food we eat is rather sweet or sour, but once again, the mind allows us to enjoy a good meal.

The cover that protects us can help us identify if we are touching something or someone, but it is the mind that makes us enjoy a caress.

We can, therefore, conclude that the product human being is designed to learn in an almost unlimited manner, to remember all it has learnt in the past, to establish a field of knowledge that interacts with new experiences; we can enjoy beauty, feel the music, delight our senses with scents and tastes, get emotional when someone kisses us and laugh heartily. In addition, this product has the capability to create and imagine non-existent situations, fantastic worlds, and pleasant experiences.

At this point, a shrewd User may start guessing that this manual could lead to utopia.

No, No AND No!

Try reading something with the curiosity and interest of a child. Do just that; do not think that you are wasting your time, or that you should be checking your bank account or taking your car for a revision instead. Write down on a piece of paper what you notice from the book, and you will see how you don't forget what you've learnt.

In the same way, sit and eat. Just eat. Smell your food deeply, put a small piece inside your mouth and pass it over the receptors. Feel the texture, the temperature, the different tastes of it... Watch how, even a simple piece of bread can offer you endless sensations!

Try and do the same with everything in your life, and you will finally understand that the product human being is designed to enjoy all what surrounds it.

I know; in a world like ours, we do not have time for these things.

So, what do we have time for?

The question comes from someone who has spent years constantly running up and down, doing one thing while he was thinking of all the other things he should be doing, instead. It's me.

There is no way we can enjoy anything if we are not present, physically and mentally. There's no point hearing how awesome a party was if you didn't go.

But I know that you, Mr. User, do not believe everything you read in this book, and that you perhaps the question of pain and suffering comes to your mind.

Yes, the product human being can perceive positivity and negativity with the same intensity, although sometimes it seems that the negative weighs more.

Have you ever been sick?

Have you ever had a terrible toothache in the middle of the night?

The pain and fever stop you thinking clearly; time goes slowly and, and no matter how hard you try, you can't relax and fall asleep.

And what happens when the pain is over, and the fever disappears?

You walk out of the house and everything seems lighter; the flowers are more colourful, and food tastes amazing... Because after suffering, the product human being needs to enjoy, to be present. That moment, it is not the time to put the mind on automatic pilot. And this is the reason bad things seem to be more intense than good things: most of the time when we are not suffering, we function with the mind on automatic pilot.

At this point we have glimpsed the multitude of benefits the product human being can offer thanks to its visible components, but the presence of the invisible component Mind, power them to almost unimaginable levels.

But what about the other invisible component? Don't we have enough with what we have?

Well, we could live without our Essence, but we would be zombies.

It is true that there are many specimens in operation that seem to lack something: THE ESSENCE. However, that is impossible because all products are manufactured with all its components without exception. The Essence may be discharged, minimized, cornered, subjugated; but it's there.

ESSENCE

The Essence seems to be the true identity of the human being, which gives meaning to the rest of the product. The true `Me'. The one we saw as a component in the mind is the false `Me', which is not that it is so false. The true `Me' would come to be the big BOSS and the `Me' that dwells in the mind: his secretary.

It is quite hard to define the component Essence, because it has a unique energy and, at the same time, it cooperates with a bigger system (check the Net work section for more information). It would be quite right to say that the human being has a tiny part, a spark, of that being that which many call God; and the rest of the product is designed only to serve this.

The Essence produces the creative impulse for an idea to materialize in the mind. It's what creates curiosity, which the Mind transforms into learning and knowledge.

It's the need of having memory, emotions, feelings and perceptions; it does not create them, because that is the Mind's job. Therefore, the Mind is the Essence's main tool, and the Body, its executing arm.

At this point, you may be doubting, with reason, what I am saying. Particularly, if you are a pragmatic person. However, if a neurosurgeon such as Wilder Penfield, believed in the Soul or Essence, surely this tells us something[3]. Add to that, scientists from Dresden (Germany), claim to have weighed it[4], also Dr. Konstantin Korotkov[5] has photographed the soul while leaving the body.

How is it that the human being accepts the existence of the Mind without hesitation but has no clear beliefs when when it comes to the Essence?

This was partially answered when we talked about the definition of Mind and its attributes:

---

[3] Wilder Penfield, (1891 – 1976) Neurosurgeon who contributed important advances to the study of neurological mechanisms and to the development of neurosurgery.
[4] The scientific magazine Horizon published the experiments that assure that the human soul weights around 21 grams.
[5] Konstantin Korotkov G., Ph.D., Deputy Director of Saint-Petersburg Federal Research Institute of Physical Culture. Professor of Computer Science and Biophysics at Saint-Petersburg Federal University of Informational Technologies, Mechanics and Optics.

"The level of consciousness seems to be a border over which Mind or Essence, may have control".

If the level of consciousness is controlled by the Mind, the false Me is the true Me and behaves as such. If consciousness is in power of the Essence, the Mind knows that there is someone more important than it, whom it must obey.

I think it would be better understood if we explain it as if we have two people dwelling within us.

Do you remember the story of the two wolves?

One night an old Indian Cherokee told his grandson the story of a battle taking place inside each person. He said: "Within each of us there is a hard battle between two wolves. One of them is an evil wolf, violent, full of anger and aggression. The other is all kindness, love, joy and compassion". The grandson spent a few minutes thinking about what his grandfather had told him and finally asked him: "Tell me, grandfather, which one of the two wolves will win?" And the old Indian replied, "The one you feed"

I'm not sure if it's really like this. But I am sure that there are Essences with more energy than others, and that the more energy, the greater capacity of the Mind.

The Happiness.
User's manual for humans

OPERATIVE SYSTEM

We will use the term 'operative system' for the group of components which manages resources and provides services to facilitate the harmonic functioning of the product. That is, the system which helps human beings achieve their objectives.

What a definition, ah?

But it's not as complicated as it sounds. It is, more or less, the definition of any machine's operative system, like a car. We have a product with specific components and an objectives or purpose. Of course, we need to know how the product works and its purpose before we use it.

What I mean is, if we buy a car, put the right type of fuel in it, put the key in the ignition, turn it on, engage the clutch, put it in gear, release the clutch and accelerate…, the car will take us where we want to go. That is, assuming that we know where we want to go.

And now, dear User, you are saying: "This man is stupid! Anybody can start a car."

My answer to that is this short story…

Hermenegildo Solís was a shepherd. He lived in a small village lost in the mountains. He had a simple life until one day luck smiled on him and, he won the lottery.

— *You must buy a car* — *said his friend, Anacleto.*

— *What for?* — *asked Hermenegildo, who would never have thought of doing such a thing.*

— *All the important people have a car... or two!* — *explained Anacleto.*

So, without a second thought, Hermenegildo went down to the big city, and bought the most modern and expensive car he could find.

One month later, his friend came up to visit him and asked him if he had bought the car.

— *Yes, I bought it! And it is wonderful!*

Then, he spent an hour and a half explaining all the things he loved about his new car.

— *At night, the lights turn on automatically... If it rains, the windscreen wiper starts without touching any button... The trunk opens when you approach it, and a woman greets you by name when you sit in the driver's place... Also, the steering wheel and the seat automatically adjust position to your height and weight...*

— *And have you been anywhere?*

— *No, I don't know how to drive!*

Like Hermenegildo, we have spectacular equipment, but we misuse it or we use it just to entertain ourselves.

Because of this, and in light of all the mistakes I've made in my life, I've tried to reflect on our operative system and its optimal functioning. The most important or relevant part in this case is the software. That's to say, the invisible components. And of those the conductor of the orchestra is undoubtedly, the Essence.

The Essence establishes priorities, generates impulses, motivates emotions and demands perceptions. Within it, there is the true identity as, it is the only one who knows the meaning of life. The Mind, which is the other part of the software, should be subordinate to the Essence; it should be silent, obedient, and ready to carry out the Essence's orders without challenging them. For its part, the Mind should pass the order it receives to the rest of the team (the visible components), to enable the product to reach its goals.

Let us look at a working example:

In a big company, the manager has the control. After establishing the general objectives and the lines of action, he gives his colleagues the responsibility of achieving the desired results. This is why managers surround themselves with specialists. These specialists interpret the orders given and transmit them to the rest of the team, who organize the tasks, the timing, resources, and designate assignments to the appropriate worker.

This is common sense. But…

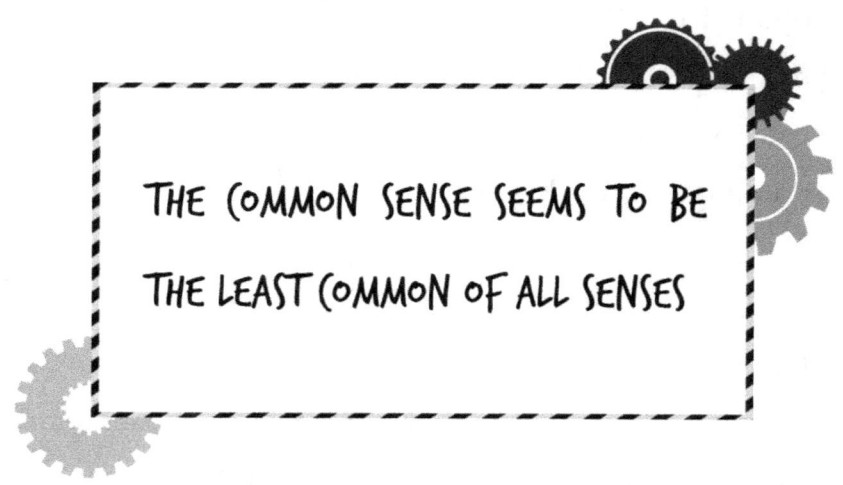

THE COMMON SENSE SEEMS TO BE THE LEAST COMMON OF ALL SENSES

I have seen general managers trying to teach the production team how to do their job.... And people working in intermediate positions, pretending to be more than the general manager.

— Instead of nuts and bolts we should make parasols.

I know this sounds ridiculous. It is extremely difficult that managers, despite all their training, could operate a machine better than an experienced machinist.

And at the same time, a foreman would not understand market trends as well as the general manager.

Now, let us imagine that the Mind wants to teach the liver how to use the bile. When the liver is built for this. That's its job!

Even so, how many people do we know that when they are worried, have liver problems?

A personal anecdote:

Few years ago, I was working for a leading European company. Everything went well, until the managers started putting extra pressure on the foremen. It was not a logical kind of pressure; it did not have anything to do with achieving specific goals for the company. It was, actually, what it is nowadays called *mobbing*[6] or *bossing*[7]. Most of the specialists working in the company decided to quit. I am quite tough, but one day I suddenly started to feel dizzy at work. By the weekend, I was still dizzy and my neck was painful. I decided to go to the doctor. My blood pressure was sky high, even though I have always had a strong tendency to faint due to low blood pressure.

The analysis they took showed that my body functions were a mess.

---

[6] *Mobbing:* to bully or harass.
[7] *Bossing:* harassment at work, which includes psychological violence towards the employees, intended to produce fear, disdain or discourage among the workers.

From that day on, they filled me with pills; for the blood pressure, for the cholesterol, for anxiety and acidity... I lived like that, until one day, I quit my job. Nowadays, my blood pressure is normal and my cholesterol too and I don't even need to take aspirins.

How is it possible that the nervous system can twist and turn our body in such a way?

This is because the Mind has power over the nervous system.

But who has power over the Mind?

The external dangers do -regardless if they are real or apparent.

That's to say, when the Mind believes that is the general manager, the fake *Me* -the Ego- takes the spot of the Soul. Then, the product *human being* stops working harmonically. It would be the same if we put a secretary in the position of a boss.

The position is too overwhelming, for the *Ego*. It does not know what to do, and it starts running around and searching the past for answers, flying ahead imagining solutions. It's not in the present, which is where it should be.

All right, in theory this is very simple.

I agree.

In fact, my Mind has always been my biggest nightmare.

When I was thirteen or fourteen, my parents made me take a psychological test, which measured intelligence and career orientation. The results showed a brilliant IQ and a highly abstract intelligence. Do you know what that means?

Having that kind of Mindset is like having a car that can reach a high speed quickly, but that stops all the time to check its surroundings. Everything distracts it, everything catches its attention, and it is near impossible for it to focus on the thing that it should: racing.

I have concluded that the operative system of human beings is designed in a very harmonic manner. If you have an Essence or Soul with a lot of energy, it follows to have a very powerful Mind, and a strong body. On the other hand, an Essence with low energy levels will have a weak Mind and a less powerful body. These are not unfair factory settings, but rather common sense: a weak Mind under a corresponding Essence is capable of achieving much more than a strong, hyperactive Mind running around under no control.

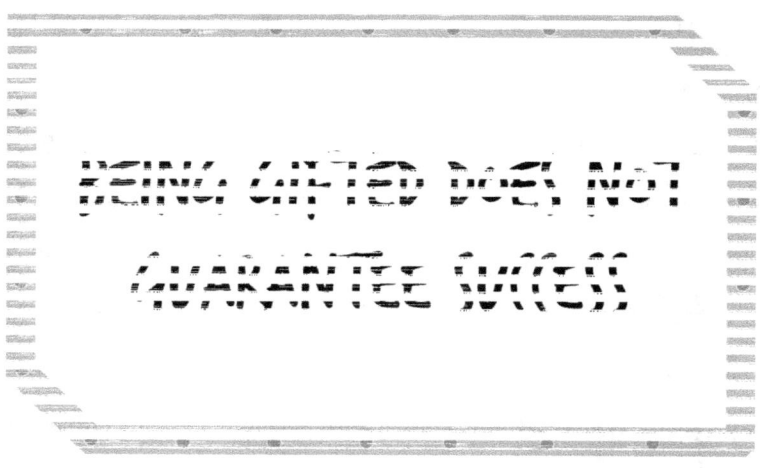

Here is another story to illustrate my point:

Peter and John wanted to be tennis players from when they were really young. Peter was a little short for his age, and tended to gain weight easily. John was tall and had an athletic build. Peter's parents didn't have the money to send him to a tennis course, nor to buy him a tennis racket. John's parents were members of the most prestigious Tennis Club in town, and they bought him a racket as soon as he could hold one with both hands. John used to play with his dad or his brother while dreaming of being a famous tennis player, winning competitions, raising trophies and signing balls. Peter, on the other hand, made do by watching tennis matches on TV, and practising with a ping pong bat and a ball he had got for Christmas, against the wall.

When John was 8 years old, his parents hired a tennis instructor for him. He taught him all the techniques and advised him to keep training and practising every day. John practised two or three hits, and then he would go to have a soda; two or three more and he wanted an ice cream. He was not consistent, but he still dreamt that he would become an international tennis player.

As Peter loved watching tennis on TV so much, his uncle decided to give him his old wooden tennis racket and a new set of tennis balls. For Peter, this was the best gift ever. The back wall of their house was testimony of his dream and soon his parents were replacing broken windows regularly, their own and the neighbours. One day, Peter's dad explained to him that to be a good tennis player it would be better to have an athletic body and money to pay for good equipment and a good trainer.

— Even if you had all of that, the probability of achieving in such a competitive sport, is very low — his father told him — . I think you should study for a good career.

Peter was sad, but he did not stop practising against the wall, every day. He started eating less, and soon began losing weight. And because he felt lighter and more agile, he started practising even more, and teaching himself techniques he found on the internet.

He practised so often and with so much enthusiasm that he soon stopped breaking windows.

At the same time, knowing his parents were making a big effort so he could study, he didn't let his studies slip.

His parents saw that there was no way they would be able to convince him to stop obsessing over tennis, so they found a club in the neighbourhood and signed him up to take classes with other kids. Peter's happiness was complete; he anxiously awaited the end of classes so he could go to train. The other kids made fun of his old racket, but he did not care; he hit the ball even harder every time they made a joke. One day, his racket broke, and so did his world. His coach saw him crying and decided to lend him one of his own rackets. To his surprise, he discovered Peter had a spectacular back hand.

John was still dreaming to become a famous tennis player, but he started skipping his classes and only practised occasionally. It was in vain that his parents bought him the latest design, graphite racket and top of the range shoes, he always came up with new excuses to skip his training classes. Regardless, he still won some trophies with his Club. After all, he was tall, knew how to use the racket and had been playing since he was very young. His parents had a glass cabinet made to exhibit his medals and trophies.

Peter's coach discovered that despite the impeccable back hand and a powerful right slam, he was not good enough at serving. He was too short, so he needed to jump to serve, which made him unstable. Against all this, Peter never gave up on a single match, and fought each set like a lion. Peter's coach told him of this weakness, so Peter practised until he was serving in his dreams.

Peter competed for the first time when he was 10 and won. He started playing in the regional league, and kept winning. By the time, he was 12; he was competing against older kids.

John continued dreaming of becoming a famous tennis player, and every now and again he would take his racket from its case and swipe the air with it...

This is a tale and not the story of real persons.

If you like sport, I'm going to name two cases — one old, and the other more modern. We'll start with the older: Johnny Weissmüller, well-known for his Tarzan movies and the TV shows of Jungle Jim[8]. Johnny suffered poliomyelitis (infantile paralysis), and he recovered when he was 13 years old. The doctors advised him to swim to help recover his damaged muscles. He went on to become a competition swimmer.

The more recent case is that of football player Lionel Messi, who was diagnosed with a growth hormone deficiency as a child. I don't think I need to explain his story, much less his success.

---

[8] **Johnny Weissmüller (1904 - 1984)** was a Hungarian-born American competition swimmer and actor, best known for playing Tarzan in films of the 1930s and 1940s and for having one of the best competitive swimming records of the 20th century. Weissmuller was one of the world's fastest swimmers in the 1920s. After retiring from competitions, he became the sixth actor to portray Edgar Rice Burroughs's ape man, Tarzan, a role he played in twelve motion pictures.

If we move on to science, Albert Einstein was an introverted child who had problems expressing himself. When he was 15 years old, his teacher, Dr. Joseph Degenhart, told him he was useless and good for nothing.

Thomas Alva Edison was told by his teacher when he was only 8 years old that he was completely unproductive and lacked skills. He earnt his living selling newspapers, veggies, butter, and fruits until he had success.

There are millions of examples like these, and several movies use this type of story as their plot: the useless, stupid, or weak person who transforms into someone important, successful and rich.

It always works. People love seeing how someone normal achieves something extraordinary. Maybe this plot is so successful because it rarely happens in real life.

My message here is that perseverance —and sometimes even stubbornness— seems to give results. But of course, in the movies, there is always a stroke of luck from nowhere that helps the main character to achieve his or her dreams.

I do believe that, when the *human being* works harmoniously and in line with the visible and invisible components, listening to the Essence, the product can achieve amazing things. Plus, the whole Universe conspires to make it possible.

Oh, if only I had seen this many years ago as clearly as I do now!

But it's never too late. Not for me, and certainly not for you.

Now here's the million-dollar question:

How do we know if we are working harmoniously with our Essence?

In most cases, people think they already are, or this is how life is. Some people toe the line applying this quote:

SOME ARE BORN WITH A STAR
AND OTHERS, SHUTTERED...

This saying means that we are all born different. As you might know by now, I do not believe so.

I remember a conversation I had many years ago with a couple of hare Krishna followers[9].

At that time, I was managing a Garden center, and they brought me a plant called *Ocimum tenuiflorum,* which is considered by them to be sacred, and it was dying. The way they were dressed and the cloth bag hanging from their necks aroused my curiosity. When I asked about the bag, they explained to me that it contains prayer beads. Each ball corresponds to a mantra, which they recite in a low voice. I don't know if it was due to my questions or the fact that they exhaled peace and incense, but we started talking about religion, and they asked me if I believed in God. I answered that I thought so. After all, I had been a leader of three catholic groups in the past.

— And do you believe that God is unfair? — they asked, and I stood there, speechless for some moments. And then, they asked again:

— Why do you think that God allows some people to be born with a silver spoon, and other people in the most absolute misery?

— I think the mission that we all have is to look over the wall — I said.

---

[9] **Hare Krishna:** Religious group based in the Hinduism believes, which worships the God Krisna.

— And what is behind the wall? — asked one of them in a singing voice.

— I believe that there is a green meadow with majestic trees and wild flowers of many colours — I said, and it seemed they liked my description.

AT THAT MOMENT, I IMAGINED A REALLY HIGH WALL AND VARIOUS PEOPLE IN FRONT OF IT. SOME WERE ALMOST AS TALL AS THE WALL, OTHERS SHORTER WITH A STOOL AT THEIR SIDE AND OTHERS EVEN SHORTER WITH NOTHING.

— The taller ones just need to stand on tiptoe to see over the wall. Those of medium size can get up on the stool they have next to them, and the shortest ones must jump with all their strength to see anything. But what could happen is that the tall ones look down to the floor, the medium sized-people sit on the stool, and that only the shortest ones want to train their legs to look over the wall...

Do not ask me where I got this explanation from; I do not know, but I can say is that the hare Krishna left their sacred plant with me to be saved, and if possible to propagate more.

The most normal thing in life, contrary to what is shown in the movies, is seeing how a person who has everything in his favour, doesn't succeed.

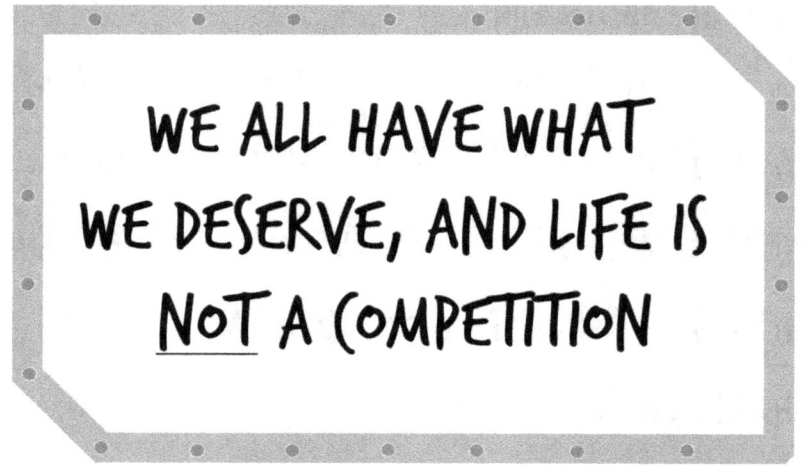

WE ALL HAVE WHAT
WE DESERVE, AND LIFE IS
NOT A COMPETITION

The million-dollar answer: we know we are functioning harmoniously when we are conscious of who we are and what we have.

And, who are we?

We are something unequalled, product of an almost unique perfection of the Universe.

And what do we have?

We have a very sophisticated body, a highly-developed mind and an Essence which is the true identity of them both.

Is it that simple?

It is.

We just need to put the right fuel in, start the engines and head towards our goal.

I imagine some of the readers thinking:

"He is saying these things because he has been lucky!"

Instead of answering you, I am going to tell you a Chinese tale:

"There once was a man breaking stones at the side of the road, it was almost midday and the sun scorched the ground. The stone cutter cried bitterly at his cruel destiny.

'What bad luck I have' he repeated like a mantra.

'All my life under this relentless sun, deformed hands from using the hammer and chisel all day, and not a drop of water to wet my parched lips.'

Suddenly he heard a voice and thought he was hallucinating.

'I see 'said the voice 'you are not content with your destiny'

'Would you be content with this job?' asked the stone cutter.

'I'll grant you a wish' replied the voice.

The man raised his bloodshot eyes and pointed to the sun.

'I want to be like him.'

'So, it shall be 'said the voice, and the stone breaker was transformed into the sun.

From high up the stone breaker transformed into the sun enjoyed his enormous power: burning crops, evaporating lakes and starting fires in forests...

But one day he realized that he was losing strength. Something was coming between his rays and the earth. Try as he could he couldn't move the clouds.

'The sun is not as powerful as the clouds, I want to be a cloud' he exclaimed.

'So, it shall be 'said the voice, and the stone breaker was transformed into cloud.

But the wind then started to blow and the stonebreaker transformed tinto cloud was blown around however the wind wanted.

'The wind is more powerful than the clouds,' he shouted indignantly, 'I want to be the wind.'

'So, it shall be,' said the voice and transformed the stonebreaker into the wind.

'At last,' he said and blew and blew, he travelled the earth starting hurricanes. There was nothing more powerful than the wind... Except the mass of water below, which he used to form waves. The more he blew, the more imposing the sea became.

'The sea is more powerful than the wind, I want to be the sea!'

So, he was transformed into the sea.

The sea was incredible, all men respected it. It could swallow up a boat in the blink of an eye and it was so huge it couldn't see itself. When the sea was angry it could wash away the sand from the shores or hit the land destroying everything. The stonebreaker was really happy with his choice: there was nothing more powerful than the sea.

One evening the stonebreaker transformed into the sea decided to remove a cliff from the face of the earth. He summoned up enormous waves and threw them against the rocks time after time until he was exhausted. After such the onslaught, he had only managed to break off some fragments of the hard rock.

'Who dares defy the sea?' he demanded, and the rocks seemed to laugh in his face.

'The rocks are harder and more powerful than the sea, I want to be rock!' he shouted offended and the voice a bit tired of so much changing, answered:

'So, it shall be.'

The stonebreaker was transformed into rock and displayed his hardness and beauty. Nor the sun, or the wind, or the clouds, or the sea could overcome him. But one day, dozy from the sun and swaying with the waves, he felt a terrible pain.

'Something is uprooting me!' He cried desperately.

'There's someone more powerful than rock and I want to be like him!' he exclaimed, and the voice sadly answered:

'and so, it shall be.'

And the stonebreaker who had been converted into sun, cloud, wind, sea and rock returned once again to be a stone cutter."

CONSIDER WHAT YOU HAVE
AND WHO YOU ARE AND MAKE
IT WORK....

The Happiness.
User's manual for humans

ACCESSORIES

The accessories are all the parts the operative system learns to use to reach its goal of happiness, easily. Here you can make your own list, if you want:

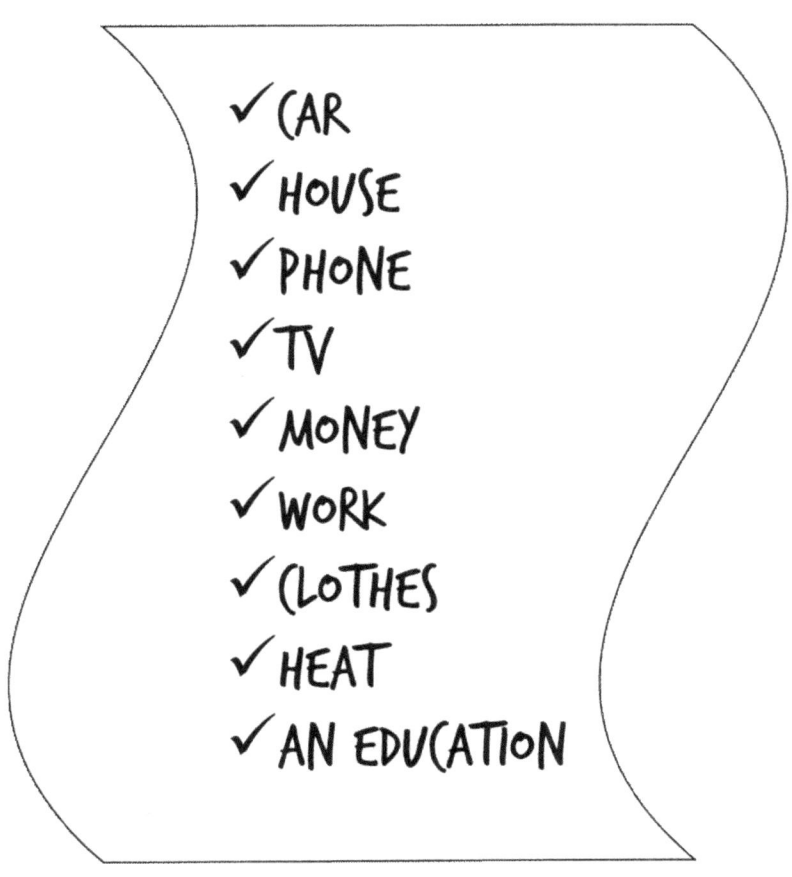

There are millions of things we can own as accessories! But they are still *just* accessories; even though advertising campaigns are obstinate in telling us otherwise.

Having a house, or two, cannot be the final goal of the product *human being*. Not even a 50-million-dollar house.

Having a car is useful for getting around, but it is definitely not something that will make us happy. Maybe, it will make us be satisfied for few days, until it starts getting old or damaged.

Having a lot of money or a good job can be very satisfactory, but those things are just accessories to achieve goals; not a goal in itself.

Giving a mere accessory the responsibility of making such a complex, perfect and powerful operative system reach its goal is plain stupid.

But, how many of us are ready to spend our lives running after getting them?

Don't answer that.

What I can assure you is that those who have reached owning these accessories are no closer to achieving happiness than you or me. Sometimes they are even further away.

Through gritted teeth you could say:

— Ha! If I had money, I would have so much fun...

And I can tell you that you are only saying that because you do not have it.

Apart from rare exceptions, those who have a lot of money usually fear losing it, and look for ways of making even more money in case they lose what they have.

IT'S EASY TO RISE, IT'S THE FALL THAT HURTS.

Am I saying we should be poor to be happy?

Absolutely not!

What I'm saying is, we should never confuse the means with the goal. That's to say that any material thing we have gets old, gets broken or becomes outdated. They are accessories, not goals and should be given the relevant amount of importance in our life.

If we reduce our goal as human beings to obtaining accessories, it will become a never-ending circle. There will always be a new model to reach.

Another short story for you:

Simon had it all: sophisticated cars, a jet-ski, a yacht. He even owned a beach house, an apartment building and several houses in the country.

It was a great feeling to be able to organize parties for friends, and surprise them with champagne and banquets at home.
He also loved entering a restaurant and instantly getting the VIP table.

Well-being, comfort and security were the three pillars of his life, and he thought he could not be happier.

Simon woke up realizing he was drooling. He did not want to open his eyes, because in a flash he remembered… He tried to put his hands under the pillow and feel the soft sheets around his body. Instead, he found his own jacket folded under his head, and he felt the hay under him was his bed. He wanted to stretch and then he realized that his whole body was painful, as if somebody had been hitting him all night.

It made sense as… He had been travelling for 24h, between airports and flights, then an eight-hour train journey, and a whole day riding a mule.

He even felt like he had a fever …

The door opened with an annoying creak from the rusty hinge. A frozen draught hit his face. The figure walking towards him was holding a lamp with a little flame inside. In the darkness, Simon could only see the reflection of the light against a white silhouette.

He was the same man that had received him the night before; a leathery bag of skin and bones, limping and blind in one eye, but with amazing energy. He brought a glass of warm milk and a piece of rice bread, for Simon. He spoke in a very low voice, but it didn't matter, Simon wouldn't have understood even if he'd yelled, as he spoke a language he had never heard before. The man smiled as he spoke, and Simon could see that the few teeth he had left were mustard-yellow.

'The Master will receive you tomorrow in the afternoon' a bearded young man translated into English for him, from the straw mattress at his side. And added: 'You are either very important or are in deep trouble, for them to give you preference…'

Simon thought that in a different time it would be because he was important, but now it was because he was in trouble.

When Ellen, his beloved wife, first started having symptoms, neither of them gave it much importance. A bottle of good champagne and some oysters with lemon, solved the problem. The second attack forced her to the hospital. The doctors could not find anything wrong, and recommended a special diet. The third attack came unexpected, like a wolf that has been hiding in the forest, attacking very quickly. Pancreatic cancer, surgery too late, and fast advancing disease… He had a hard time watching her die… with morphine and other drugs…her eyes were huge, tired and defeated. He had so much pain inside that he would cut down all the trees in the world, to avoid their green promise of hope after catastrophe.

But if he thought that was the worst of it, he was wrong.

Ellen's ashes were still warm, and the image of her pleading eyes was still fresh in Simon's mind when the stock market went down for three consecutive weeks. A false rumour sank his signature company. His daughter asked him via a lawyer, for half her mother's inheritance.

Simon's friends disappeared as quickly as the cars, houses and yachts he sold.

He was ruined without knowing why.

Somebody told him about a Master who lived in Tibet, who could perform miracles but who was also very hard to find. Simon invested all he had left in finding him.

So, there he was, in that inhospitable place, mountains above and savannahs below, without really knowing if his dream was real or if reality was just a dream.

He spent his day waiting, watching the sheep without seeing them, and seeing people without looking at them…

The Master had the same curious form as the servant. He hid an amazing agility under his cloak and attentively listened to Simon's troubles. He shared Simon's torture, relived with him Ellen's death and saddened himself on hearing of Simon's financial and family problems, helping Simon to put them into perspective.

This enlightened Master sat next to Simon suffering with him, in front of them a small window looked out on to the immense landscape. And Simon thought that there in that place, nobody needed a yacht, an expensive house or a car with automatic parking and leather seats… and wondered if Ellen's wide open eyes were due to her seeing that also…

— This shall pass, my son, this shall pass… — said the master, tactically closing the cycle and clearly closing the door, on his nose.

So, Simon went back home, defeated and not really convinced about the Master's words.

He lamented on spending so much money — the last he had — on travelling to Tibet, but he admitted to himself that it was done, and nothing could change that.

So, he started to build his life again, and his daughter came back to him, bringing his granddaughter along, who had the same eyes as Ellen. The apartment next to him was rented by an attractive artist with lots of talent. She only needed a little push to become a celebrity. And the best part was, she wanted to sleep with him.

It is hard to say how Simon felt at that point. He went from the living dead to being alive again. He recovered his money; he loved again, and was being loved in return, and he had his daughter by his side again. He still remembered the Master's words; he was right, and Simon was thankful for it.

Simon travelled again; took several flights, the long train trip and the mule — which seemed to be the same one — . He arrived late at night so he stayed again with the old man who had received him the first time.

These were two situations, both the same and opposite. The first time, he could have died and didn't care; his pain was so great. This time, didn't mind living forever.

The old master received him again under his heavy cloak. He looked into his eyes while Simon told him how thankful he was. He opened his mouth, smiled, and repeated the only phrase he knew in English:

— This shall pass, my son… this shall pass …

Remember this phrase:

"THIS TOO SHALL

PASS"

It is true that the world is organized in such a way that if we don't have money or a job, it seems like we have nothing at all, and therefore are nobody. Too often, we think of ourselves in terms of the accessories we have, instead of how close we are to obtaining our happiness.

It is also true that fighting the system is not useful. It has been done in the sixties, and the phrase "Peace and love" has left some interesting symbols, addiction to LSD and quite good music, but apart from that, nothing else remains of it.

In my opinion, revolutions are made from the inside out, starting with ourselves.

Don't ask society to change; change yourself first!

Here I can't resist the temptation to add:

"CHANGE, AND YOU WILL EXPERIENCE THE THRILL OF DISAGREEING WITH HALF OF HUMANITY!"

The Happiness.
User's manual for humans

POTENTIAL

I think we all know what the potential of something is. It is the intrinsic capability to reach an effect or goal under certain conditions.

Let us take for example a waterfall. The water at the top has the potential to fall from the top to the bottom. As it falls, it gains speed and loses height. This means that it loses potential energy, and it gains kinetic energy. If at the bottom there is a generator, all that kinetic energy will be transformed into electricity.

With this example, I have simplified this explanation quite a lot. Not all potential energy transforms into kinetic energy, as not all kinetic energy becomes electricity. Most waterfalls have rocks and stones that reduce the speed of the water; many drops become steam or fog, and some of the water is diverted and doesn't reach the power generator.

The product *human being*, when it is born, has a huge potential to reach its goal of happiness. I do not need to explain this further as children are, in general, naturally

HAPPY.

It is true, until they begin to use reason around six or seven, they are normally very happy —regardless of what they have and how they are—.

However, the potential that helps them believe that they can be superheroes, does not all transform in kinetic energy. That is what society, parents and teachers are for...

... TO MAKE THEM SEE THAT IT IS NOT POSSIBLE

¡What! You mean that those responsible for making such a perfect product fail to reach its goal of happiness are others?

YES

That is horrible! Isn't it?

Before you start getting angry with the whole world, you should know that you chose them.

And you'd say: Bah! I didn't choose to be born; I didn't choose my parents.

Yes, you did, even though you are not aware of it. But we all chose to be born and we all chose our parents.

And pretty much nobody is happy with their choice (including myself).

In other words, the potential of the kinetic energy in the product human being is affected by the actions of the people he or she chose.

Am I trying to say that we self-boycott?

Not necessarily.

We can learn from a person or a situation, and gain or lose energy. It all depends on us, and this mechanism is called free will.

The problem is that free will depends on our level of consciousness. If our level of consciousness is controlled by the Mind, it will take an apparently negative event as an aggression, and will prepare to react accordingly. If our consciousness is in the Soul or Essence, an order will be sent to the Mind to analyse what happened from an objective perspective; there will be no reaction but rather a tendency to defend the product human being or file the situation as an experience.

I said this before:

"It would be right to say that the product human being contains a tiny part, or a spark, of that who some call God, and the rest of this marvellous product is manufactured exclusively to serve that spark."

And now, I would like to go even further.

I actually believe that we all are potential gods. Reusing the example of the waterfall, our free fall of life will put rocks in our path, a lot of our energy will evaporate and we may miss the generator at the bottom... Regardless, we have extra energy and equipment to achieve our goal; that is, to be happy. Better still we could be happy everyday and every hour of our life.

HOW?

If we were like children. We have already said that they are usually happy.

And you would say: But we can't go backwards. We can't avoid growing up.

My answer to that is: Going forward or backwards is a matter of references. Have you never been waiting at the traffic lights and had the impression your car is rolling backwards but when you hit the break you realise it's the car next to you going forward that created this sensation.

It is exactly the same in life. If we take a child as a reference, becoming a boring, serious and sad adult means, actually, to move backwards.

If we take adults as a reference, to become one is to progress.

Allow me User, to take an example from the Bible, and more precisely, from the New Testament:

This is from Matthew, chapter 19

(13) *'Then people brought little children to Jesus for him to place his hands on them and pray for them. But the disciples rebuked them.[14] Jesus said, "Let the little children come to me, and do not hinder them, for the kingdom of heaven belongs to such as these." [15] When he had placed his hands on them and prayed, he departed.'*

This is from apostle John, chapter 3

'There was a man of the Pharisees, named Nicodemus, a ruler of the Jews: The same came to Jesus by night, and said unto him, "Rabbi, we know that thou art a teacher come from God: for no man can do these miracles that thou doest, except God be with him" (John 3:1-2).'

'Jesus answered and said unto him, "Verily, verily, I say unto thee, Except a man be born again, he cannot see the kingdom of God". Nicodemus saith unto him: "How can a man be born when he is old? can he enter the second time into his mother's womb, and be born?" Jesus answered, "Verily, verily, I say unto thee, except a man be born of water and of the Spirit, he cannot enter into the kingdom of God. That which is born of the flesh is flesh; and that which is born of the Spirit is spirit. Marvel not that I said unto thee, Ye must be born again" (John 3:3-7).'

Putting aside the religious connotations and the interpretations that each Church has given to these texts, it is evident that Jesus gave a huge importance to children, to the point of driving his supporters crazy by telling them they should become children again, otherwise, they couldn't enter his Kingdom.

Now, I suggest we play a game. Let's take the fact of growing up as an event seen from the point of reference of an adult:

1. "I must behave myself so my parents don't tell me off."
2. "I must go to school so they don't mark me as ignorant."
3. "Playing is good, but only after duty."
4. "I must do my homework so I don't get told off by my teacher and then my mother."
5. "I must clear my toys away so I can have dessert."

Then, when we reach the adolescence, which I don't understand why we call it this — and I'll explain later —:

1. "They won't let me drink as I'm not old enough."
2. "They won't let me smoke as I'm not old enough."

3. "I can't go to parties as I'm not old enough."

  "I can't fail any subjects as my parents will get angry."

And in adulthood:

1. "I must find a job if I don't want to die of hunger."

2. "I must find a partner if I don't want to be alone."

3. "I must buy a new car if I don't want to be classed as naïve."

4. "I must buy or build myself a house if I don't want to appear inferior."

5. "I must have children so no one can say I can't, or pity me."

Ok, these are just examples, but in the end, what does all the child's potential become?

IT BECOMES A STEREOTYPE.

And you may reply, with good reason:

— If it was not like this, we would not fit into society.

That is true. And submissively fitting into society *seems* to be the goal of the product we call human being.

This reminds me of a decorated tile that my grandma had in her backyard. It had the following inscription in it:

"¡EAT SHIT! MILLIONS OF FLIES CAN'T BE WRONG"

Now, let's see what happens if we take children as the point of reference for this game:

1. "I always behave myself, even though I make mistakes sometimes."
2. "I have the right to go to school to learn more, there is a whole world out there."
3. "I don't want to stop playing even if I have homework to do. But, when I do my homework I feel proud of myself."
4. "It doesn't matter if I don't clear my toys away, but I don't expect anyone else to."

And then, when we reach... I prefer to call adolescence; 'renaissance' I'll explain why later:

1. "If I drink I'll have a hangover and this will affect what I can do."
2. "If I smoke I can't play sport."
3. "If I go to a party I may not like what happens there."
4. "I may fail a subject or more, but I give my best to see where my limits are."

And, finally, when we become adults:

1. "Work is good for learning and paying my way, but I'll find something that satisfies me."

2. "I can live alone or with my partner, which ever is better for me."

3. "A house is the place where I can be myself."

4. "A car is something to carry me from one place to another, and if it's new it will give me less problems."

5. "I would like to have people around me so we can learn from each other."

Can you see how the game changes depending on the point of view?

In both cases, events will come up; some will be painful, and some will be good.

BUT IT IS NOT WHAT HAPPENS THAT MATTERS, IT'S HOW WE FACE THOSE EVENTS.

Our attitude towards events determines whether our potential is transformed into energy or wasted.

That means: to be able to transform our potential into movement depends on our ability to see life through the eyes of a child. And our responsibility should be that no child under our care loses that way of perceiving life.

DOES THAT SEEM EASY?

As I promised, I would like to explain why I do not like the term adolescence and why I prefer the term "renaissance", instead. If you fancy it, I have written a book with that name as title.

The word *adolescence* invokes the feeling of having an inevitable sickness that only time can cure, like a cold. I do not believe that any stage in life is a sickness; more of an opportunity. That is why I would rather call the adolescent or teenage years *"renaissance"*. I believe this because during those years we wrongly call adolescence, we are reborn to face a society full of taboos, rules and impositions, morally and psychologically evolving at the speed of a mammoth.

We are reborn to contemplate our circumstances; we discover that justice, tolerance and understanding often mean the opposite of what is in the dictionary.

I have not chosen the word *"adaptability"*, because it would imply the defeatist acceptance that the world is how it is, and nothing can make it change.

If you read the definition of adolescence, you will find something like "time in which individuals develop the skills to be considered socially self-sufficient". In addition, an adolescent is described as "immature" and "childish".

Now, look around, and tell me if you agree that some people actually need to be considered as adolescents until the day they die.

I would define the *"renaissance"* as an unquantifiable period of time in which we learn to be socially independent.

It is the time in which we apply those natural qualities and skills we were born with to specific problems, and in which we analyse the values given by family and society and decide if they are to be *our* values, too.

Now that I have explained this whole topic regarding my choice of words, I want to add an element to the list of things that we need as products to transform the potential into energy and movement:

THE MIND NEEDS TO BE FOCUSED IN THE PRESENT

This seems simpler than it is.

The Mind has a gear shift with three positions: Reverse, automatic pilot and forward.

This means that there is not a neutral point: we cannot stop it at any point.

This statement comes from someone who has practiced mediation and mind control; who has read every book there is about self-help; who tried the sutras, the mantras and all Hermetic principles.

It is impossible to stop our Mind or to control it completely. The only useful thing we can do is to slow it down.

This is what meditation and mind control are for —I am not going to delve into this topic; there is already plenty of material about it, out there—. I do want to point out that many people consider that lowering the brain waves is equivalent to setting your mind on automatic pilot or being apathetic. It is not. I have always been sceptic towards how Asian masters and wise men are portrayed: they always have a very placid, peaceful look in their eyes. I do not think one can be able to remain in REM phase all day, because that would mean we are sleeping all the time. If that was our nature, we would just be like that, naturally and effortlessly.

The Mind is always occupied; even when we carry out a boring or repetitive activity. The Mind always escapes to imaginary situations located in the future, or to memories from the past. Even when we meditate, the mind is still busy. It does slow down, it relaxes and it focuses on one point only, but it is still active. That is all right; that's its function.

What I'm talking about is the mind being active but only in the present. Its enormous ability for organization, problem solving and activity planning transforms potential into moving energy.

And how do we do this?

We put the mind in the service of the Soul and making it clear that the Soul is in charge.

Again, how do we achieve that?

You need to realize who you are and what you have.

At this point, you can return to page 20 and start reading again from that page, going in circles for years…

…OR YOU CAN CONTINUE READING, LEAVING ANY PRECONCEPTIONS BEHIND.

NETWORKING

Until now, I have talked about the product *human being* as an individual. And even though I earlier said that other human beings can affect our energy, it was a circumstantial mention.

The reality is that the product *human being* works independently but at the same time it connects with other products. And by *connect* I do not refer to physical contact, necessarily.

You might say:

—In our century, this is true. We have lots of forms of communication and open channels thanks to globalization. But what about before?

Before it was, in essence, the same.

A detail I always find fascinating is that in the Palaeolithic age, the use of the arrowhead starts at the same time in each of the four continents and among completely different ethnic groups. It was probably the same with fire. It is true that the human being was quite nomadic at the time, but even so moving took quite a long time. So, could it be that the simultaneous appearance of ideas was due to another cause than the nomadic lifestyle?

Another interesting topic regarding networking is the existence of celebrations and dancing. Both involved more than one person.

It seems that it could be a telepathic communication between all products, or at least, between tuned products.

And now you say: — That is pure speculation...

Not really. Neurologists have discovered that the brain (which I call the central computer) has some neurones call *mirror*. These neurones are in charge of learning by imitation and the responsible for empathy. This means that being happy when others are happy, or suffering because they are is due to these nervous cells. This is scientifically proven, and now scientists are investigating the possibility of connecting mirror neurones with other neurones to see if communication and exchange is possible.

Personally, I do not need them to prove the latter, since I have had many experiences that prove that it is possible.

I'm now going to share two stories with you:

In 2002 I was invited to a Bonsai congress in Spain. At the time, I was living in Argentina. That event was very important for me, because it determined my decision to move to Europe permanently.

The main problem was that I needed to renew my passport, and at those times, a huge part of the Argentinian population wanted to flee the country due to the economic crisis, the insecurity and the *corralito*[10]. I had all the paperwork completed in time and I even bought my tickets to Spain, but the passport was taking too long. Every week, I would go to the Police station to ask about it, and they always gave me the same answer: "It will be here soon".

I remember that, just to ask if it had arrived, you had to queue for hours. Time was running out for me, and I did not have a valid passport.

A week before my trip, I was sure I wouldn't be able to travel. Despite this I went again to the police station, but this time I went around closing time, instead of in the morning, as I had done on other occasions.

I was surprised to see that there was no queue, and I remember thinking that it was probably a holiday.

But no, the doors were open even though there was no one in the reception. A bit disconcerted I started to look around.

---

[10] **Corralito**: In Argentina, restriction of the free disposal of cash imposed by the government in December 2001. Due to the popularity that the term acquired, it began to be used in all the Spanish-speaking countries to refer to the immobilization of deposits Made by the government of any country.

It was definitely not normal. I was about to leave when a man with a white uniform came into the office.

I must point out that Police officers wear blue; but this uniform was white and it had golden epaulettes. I am not familiar with the police hierarchy so I am not sure of his rank. When he saw me there he came over and very politely asked me if he could help me with anything. This was a sharp contrast to the usual dry:'what do you want'. So, I gladly started to explain all the problems I was having trying to get my passport, when another officer with the usual blue uniform interrupted me:

—I can take care of this, Sir —he said, referring to me, and I then understood that the blue uniform was of lower rank than the white one.

—No, I'll carry on —answered the man in white.

I was freaking out abit, but tried to explain the situation as well as I could. I didn't have much time, and I needed to know if my passport would arrive or if I needed to change my flight.

After listening to me carefully, he said:

—Listen up, now you are going to take the first bus going to Buenos Aires, and go to this address—he wrote it down on a piece of paper— *and don't leave there until they give you your passport. Trust me, you cannot let one more day pass.*

He handed me the paper with the address, said goodbye and returned to the offices. When I arrived home, I told my wife and she said that maybe that was some kind of sign, so I should at least try. It was a Thursday, and to go to Buenos Aires to sort out paperwork on a Friday was bold. I went anyway. When I arrived at the address, there was such a long queue that I thought I should maybe give up. After waiting for an hour, without moving a metre, a lady dressed in blue started giving out numbered papers. She did not let me explain my situation.

—Is it to pick up? —she asked cuttingly, and I answered nodding my head.

—Come with me —she said, and she took me all the way up to the entrance.

—Stay here —she ordered, while she pointed at a group of twenty people who were waiting there. I had no time to ask anything before a door opened and they let us in.

—Go up the stairs and wait on the first floor—said another man, and we all ran upstairs.

In half an hour we'd all been seen, and they told me I could pick up my passport the next day. `On a Saturday? ', I thought, but since the whole situation had been strange, I didn't want to question anything.

As I had no money to pay for a hotel, I asked a friend if I could stay at her place that night. When I explained to her what had happened, she told me that they were taking the mickey, as all public offices are closed at weekends. Regardless, the next day I went back to the building. Logically, as just as my friend had told me, everything was closed!

I don't think that I've ever felt so stupid in my entire life. But even then, I still walked up and down the street, expecting something to happen. Maybe I was hoping for a miracle.

When I was about to give up, I saw another man, just as lost and confused as me, who was checking all the doors with a paper in his hand. It was consoling to know I was not the only idiot in the world.

We looked at each other, and he asked:

— Did they also tell you...?

— Yes —I answered, knowing we were in the same situation

— But everything is closed…

— Yes —I repeated.

In that moment, a young man crossed the street and yelled:

—This way!

The door was not the same we had used the day before. Moreover, it was closed when I walked in front of it, but it actually led to the same floor we had been on the day before.

In half an hour, we both had our passports.

—This is the strangest thing that has even happened to me, but thank God, because my flight leaves tomorrow—he said visibly moved.

—Mine is next week.

This is a true story, and some might call it coincidence. I do not.

The second story is much simpler than the first one, but nevertheless as intriguing.

For many years, I travelled 300 km. once or twice a week from Rosario to Buenos Aires. The return was always at night after all day buying plants from botanical farms. I think I already said that I used to work with plants.

During those trips, I used to do something that I do not recommend to anybody, because it is dangerous.

I also explained at the beginning of this book that my experience is based on solving my problems.

And one of those searches for solutions led me to practice mind control with the Silva and Bonomi methods.

During the trips, I listened to a cassette — I know, that is quite old —, and while I listened to it, I would relax while driving. In that way, the trip appeared much shorter, to me.

One of those days, I was very worried because I could not find the phone number of a construction worker I trusted a lot. I wanted to build a barbecue, and that man, called Luis, was an expert. I did not have his address, either.

The moment I started driving back, I put the cassette on as always, and I was ready to enter the alpha mode. But instead, my mind started thinking of all the places where that phone number could be; not just that, my mind visualized it. For those of you who are not familiar with this technique, it consists of imagining the thing you want to find as if it was in front of you, in all its detail.

When I came back from my trip, I found out that Luis had been in my shop and had left his phone number in case I needed it.

Again, coincidence?

I do not need to remark how much and for how long telepathy has been discussed and investigated. Some say it is a scam; some say it's an ability that some people have.

I believe that we all have it, but we are not able to use it voluntarily. Despite all, I believe that situations like the ones in the stories show how the product *human being* can function better through its relationship with other products.

Other examples of this property we all have are football matches. It is well known that when a team plays at home with the encouragement of their fans, they play better. How is it possible that the simple support of other people improves the performance of eleven individuals?

The thing is, when the product *human being* works in connection to others, its energy multiplies.

In terms of religion, one can be atheistic, but when attending a ceremony with singing or praying in groups, there is no denying one feels better. There are even people that have been cured or relieved of pain after one of these meetings.

Added to this, many human beings working together in a network can produce collective visions of things they all wish for. Maybe they are hallucinations; but maybe they are not. Honestly, I do not believe that a piece of wood can bleed, or that water can cause miracles by itself... But if many millions believe it possible, maybe their energy produces the expected effect.

Throughout history, we can see the birth of nations and empires created from a common idea, or great individual and collective deeds that have no rational explanation.

Did David kill Goliath with a slingshot?

Was it him, with the help of Jehovah or the energy of a whole town that wanted to avoid a war against the Philistines?

Throughout the ages, we have used symbols: flags, crosses, saints, to unite the *mirror* neurones of the human being towards an objective. We have also used hatred and resentment. Our mirror neurones are not aware of rights and wrongs. Their function is to look for other neurones like them, to empathize with each other.

The biggest quality of any commander is to be able to produce euphoria among people. They often give speeches in loud and energetic voices, they repeat slogans and direct everybody's energy towards an objective that has previously been set up. They don't even need to make sense. The important thing is that the mirror neurones start working in groups and that happens, only, when the leader is trusted by the people. For this reason, commanders and social leaders are often people with the «messiah complex», a state characterized by delusions of grandeur. I won't provide any names, but I'm sure you can think of some.

In the process of massification there is a loss of identity of our fake I, favouring a fake, collective Me. People recruited in this process can do things they would never dare to if they were alone. If they are separated from the group, they become social zombies.

However, there is another process that takes place in some associations, ecologist groups and volunteer organizations. In that each product -everyone- has an objective, and this attracts other individuals who have a similar set of values or ideas. The attraction is instinctive and rational at the same time. On one hand, there is the empathy that working in a network produces, which gives the security of belonging to something bigger than yourself and the certainty that the energy of the group is bigger than individual energy. Even this type of network needs one or two central computers organizing and leading the energy of the team. What they can achieve together is way greater than whatever they could reach individually.

I will put an example of my own, once more:

I started professionally in the world of Bonsai in 1983 in Rosario, Argentina.

I had been fascinated about bonsai since I was a child, but until then my experience was limited to one article in the Larousse Encyclopaedia which I had read a thousand times, and some seeds I had planted.

The opportunity to do something more serious was given to me when I started working with ornamental plants. Each season there were trees and bushes that didn't sell, but which had interesting trunks. I was an ecologist, and I would rather make bonsai with them than throw them in the trash. To do so, I had to search for information, but that was not easy at that time. Shortly after I started my little project, other human specimens with the same interest for the topic began appearing. And I am saying specimens because they were quite strange people, at least their appearance. In 1984, the movie Karate Kid[11] was released, and the interest in bonsai and martial arts multiplied in the west. Even the Spanish president at the time, Felipe Gonzalez, was a fan of this art.

Between 1987 and 1997 in Rosario, a big group of bonsai enthusiasts had grown up, they took lessons, searched for information, and even made their own tools.

---

[11] Karate Kid: American film based in the tale "Sometimes the heart of the turtle", from Japanese writer Kenzaburo Oe (1982). It originated a series of films up to 2010.

In October 1997, a friend and follower came to me with the news that he had been invited to be part of a Bonsai association that was being created in the city.

I did not want to join in the beginning, but I ended up being its leader.

In five years, it became the most important association in the country. We organized an annual exhibition for thousand of visitors with a national level competition that was the first and only of its kind. This led to improving techniques with the trees that had not been seen in thirty years. But when the central computer stops working, everything collapses. I left the country in 2002, and even today, the results we obtained then still shine although it has never been the same. My merit? Not really. The mirror neurones get used to contacting with other people's neurones in a specific way, so when the connection fails, they feel abandoned and deceived. The members of that group never forgave me for leaving them; to them, I was the main computer, the one who managed everybody's energy and channelled the objectives that each should achieve individually in order to reach the common goal.

It is the same in any group, organization, political party or association, anywhere in the world.

THAT IS WHY THE GENERATIONAL CHANGE IS ESSENTIAL

We could continue to give examples, even regarding some countries, but I do believe that it is quite clear that the product human being makes the most of its energy when working within a network. The problem is that when the fake I, in the Mind, giving way to a bigger false Me, expects a reward. And when there are no bounties, it feels insulted and betrayed.

It would be different if instead of the fake *Me* from the Mind, it was the *Me* from the Soul who sends orders to the mirror neurones. But that depends on each individual, and within a group, it is difficult to detect which Ego is giving the orders.

To make it easier, I will tell you another tale:

In the deepest forest, there was a group of disabled animals. Each of them were potentially impressive, but their limitations made them hide in the thick vegetation. The giraffe was missing a leg; the lion, its claws; the bat, its wings, and the panther, its eyes. One day, they decided that if they joined forces, they could compensate the deficiencies of each other with the capabilities of the group. The monkey was proclaimed the leader of the group, since he was only missing its tale. He organized them in a way that the giraffe could walk supported by the lion, and the panther offered help to the lion with its claws. At the same time, the lion was the panther's eyes, and the bat's radar was helped the monkey with hidden dangers in the night. The giraffe was on look-out for coming danger during the day.

For some time, the team worked perfectly, and even the rest of the animals feared the group. But one day, the lion started thinking that the panther was eating more than him because it had claws. At the same time, he started to complain about the giraffe, weighing too much and did not letting him walk freely. The panther started thinking that the lion did not choose the best prey, since most of them were thin and had almost no meat on them. The giraffe also had complained: when the lion was tracking down prey, he would make her lose her stability; and she started thinking that she did not need him, since she was actually a vegetarian and did not eat meat. After all, the only thing this group was offering her was a "leg", but she contributed so much more, walking all day and being on guard at all times.

The bat was sick and tired of eating the insects which fly around the animals that the lion and the panther had been eating; it was a miserable pay for the service he was offering with his powerful radar. And the monkey started getting annoyed that nobody did what he ordered; he did not really need them -he thought-, since he only used the giraffe's height to get some fruits to eat now and then.

At last, the group dissolved. The giraffe looked for another animal who could help her walk; the monkey found someone who could take him up to the trees. The panther looked for someone who could see for her, and the lion, for an animal with claws. Finally, the bat was accidentally eaten by the panther, who thought he was a rabbit.

MORAL OF THE FABLE: WORKING IN TEAMS IS SUCCESSFUL WHEN IT 'S MADE FROM FULL WHOLE SPECIMENS, BUT IF THE MIND IS IN CHARGE, EVERYBODY LIMPS, IS SHORT-SIGHTED, DEAF OR UNABLE TO TAKE DECISIONS

THE NETWORK OF TWO

This is probably the most popular kind of network and the most discussed topic regarding the history of the product we call *human being.*

This does not make much sense, since it should be the easiest type of networking: it only involves two components. However, it has led to thousands and thousands of poems, songs, novels, and even news.

I am not referring, in this case, to what we call *friendship.* It is similar, though, to any other type of networking, including the one depicted in the tale about the disabled animals. I am talking about the *couple*, a type of networking that, generally, generates huge expectations.

The term itself says it all. In Spanish, for example, the same term (couple) is used to define something balanced and with all parts at the same level. However, in English, it means *pair.* I would rather use the word *partner* to refer to it.

I will not go in depth about this topic, since there is already so much written material on the subject. I will just add that the product *human being* tends to attract one another; this attraction can happen between opposite genders or same genders, indifferently.

Such affinity starts in a chemical and visual way, and then continues towards physical contact. It often leads to an exchange of fluids. This stage is characterized by a lot of excitement among the visible components of the product human being, and a little or no activity in the invisible components.

If the visible components agree and accept the *product* of our interest, the Mind starts verifying that it is the right choice, by checking tastes and hobbies we share with this other human being. In the next phase, the Souls get in touch, generating a colourful explosion of joy.

The length of each phase is random, and it could happen that the first stage is never passed and therefore the second and third phases are never worked on.

To achieve a stable partner has been refered to throughout history as finding "the other half", "the blue prince or the knight in shining armor" or a "soul mate", and those concepts are as fateful as popular.

In the first case, *the other half*, it is assumed that the product human being is missing a part —a whole half, to be exact—. And this is not true; all human beings are made complete, with all the components they need. If we assume we are just half of a person, we will spend the rest of our lives looking for that *someone* who fits us perfectly.

That is very hard, considering that each product is unique.

So, why is this concept so popular?

The Mind of the product *human being* must develop a series of complex tasks throughout adulthood. To achieve this, the task of preparation during the childhood and the teenage years is undertaken with the help of teachers and parents. However, and since they do not have an instruction's manual to do so, they make some huge mistakes —or small ones—. Those responsible for this task do as well as they can, but they cannot avoid that their children's or students' Minds might be full of holes when they reach adulthood, and the network of two.

Did I just say *holes*?

Yes, holes, deficiencies. Some people have them in their self-esteem; others are emotional due to lack of love, or lack of displays of affection. Some are of safety due to overprotection and also there are those due to fear of repeating traumatic experiences.

We bring these *holes* to the network of two, and the first thing we do is to search for someone to fill them up. We feel that we are missing something, and the other product -the other person- has come to complete us.

The problem is that the hole is still there; even though we have someone covering it up. This makes the other "half" feel obliged to stay there, filling up our emotional gaps. And any obligation produces a sense of paralysis. That person feels that he or she cannot grow, and cannot modify any behaviour, out of fear to leave the other "half" exposed with all his or her holes. Overall, and either way, it all produces insecurity, sadness and resentment.

The result of this whole situation is that the relationship generally stops after the second phase, and both parts are shipwrecked.

In the second case, the one that considers the right man as the "blue prince or the knight in armor" sounds old school but it is still very popular among the feminine public.

Allow me to add here this very old joke:

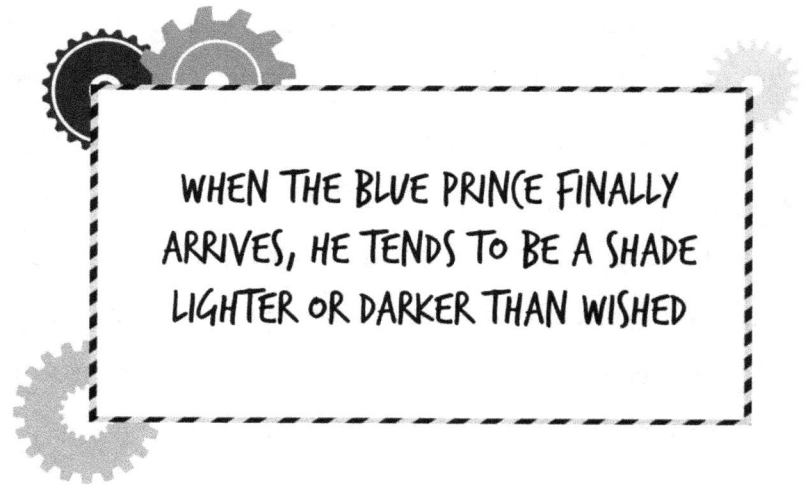

WHEN THE BLUE PRINCE FINALLY ARRIVES, HE TENDS TO BE A SHADE LIGHTER OR DARKER THAN WISHED

In real life, women who believe in finding "the perfect man", do not aspire to date a prince, but rather a multimillionaire, a Wall Street executive, a famous sportsman or a successful singer. That is, they look for a tree in whose shade they can sleep or a partner who can have them as their trophy. Who wants this? No-one in their right mind.

BEING A COUPLE MEANS WORKING TOGETHER; NOT ONE BEING THE SHADOW OF THE OTHER

Without exception, it has been the theme of the most successful novels recently.

The third example, in which partners are called "soul mates", seems to be the healthiest of them, but it is not. It's often said that opposites attract each other, and equals repel. Imagine two people who are identical: when one gets stressed, the other one gets worse. When one wants to say something, so does the other, nobody listens. When they both want to listen, no-one wants to speak. They would end up fighting, most probably.

That said from the three phrases that sum up the ideal couple it seems that none of them work, but there are many more that don't work:

Let us try to put some examples. We have Person A, and Person B. A's interests are Science, reading, sports, gardening and going to parties.

B's interests are going to the cinema, decoration of interiors, cooking, meditating and relaxing.

A and B attract each other because they are opposites, so they succeed on the first phase (physical attraction), so they start networking as a couple. But then, they discover they have no hobbies in common. When A wants to read, B turns the TV on. When B decides to start meditating, A wants to go out partying. A could give up reading and sit next to B to watch a movie, or that B decides to stop meditating to follow A to a party. But how long can these compromises last? They attract each other physically, and they maybe admire each other for their qualities and skills, but in the end, physical attraction drops. Overall, they will probably end up being just roommates.

Let us now change the situation and imagine that A keeps on having the same hobbies as before, and B shares them all. They have now not only physical attraction, but also shared hobbies and interests. This situation is perfect, is it not?

NOT REALLY.

It could be that, because they do everything together, one of them starts feeling as if they do not have their own life.

In any of these cases, the third stage (the encounter of the Souls), does not take place. The feeling of something missing intensifies and some of the parts would try to fill up the emotional holes with objects (a car, a house, a weekend house, a yacht…)

Even worse, the couple could decide to have children or to adopt a cat to compensate for what they feel missing.

So, what is the best option for a network of two? What is the best possible combination when looking for a romantic partner?

Doubtlessly, the perfect match would be having two people who share some interests but not all of them, so they can have both points in common and some freedom to develop their own life. Shared interests should create connection, not dependency. In a situation like this, they are both complete beings, not halves, so the third phase can take place. And that phase is spectacular! The common space created between the two allow them to rest and to show themselves just the way they are.

But to do so, each product —each person— needs to be aware of their own deficiencies or holes, and understand that nobody can fill them up except for himself. Both parts should have learnt to live with themselves, to enjoy their own company and to know who they are, and what they have.

There are, of course, exceptions to this case. The product *human being* is in constant evolution, and each product develops at its own pace. For this reason, when I hear somebody swearing that they will "network" with another person until the day they die, I always think that it is a risky promise. It would be great if it was that way, but the reality has proved otherwise.

However, to reach the third phase is possible and it is, without doubt, the ultimate goal for any couple. In this case, the energy of each person multiplies and obtaining the product's goal —happiness— seems much easier.

WHY ARE THERE SO MANY NETWORKS OF TWO THAT END UP IN DISASTER?

Because we put too many expectations upon the *other*.

- "You used to compensate all of my deficiencies. What am I supposed to do if you are not around? You will oblige me to take care of myself with my own limitations, my fears and all my insecurity. That hurts."

- "I used to live very peacefully under your wing. If you leave me, I will feel unprotected from life's harshness."

- "You used to be my ideal match, my love... and you deceived me."

- "You were mine, and a part of me; if we separate, I will never be myself again."

The only option to reach success as a couple or a network of two is to remember that each product is perfectly complete.

I am sorry if I have not been as explicit or romantic as you wanted me to in this point, but this is a huge topic -I could write a whole new book just on that.

The Happiness.
User's manual for humans

MALFUNCTION

In this part, I will expose some of the most typical symptoms that the product *human being* exhibits during malfunction. For sure they are not all of them. But you User, can add your own symptoms to the list if you have any:

• Constant need to acquire new objects and to follow all new trends.

• Incapable of being alone.

• Perception of another person's path as easier or more authentic than ours.

• Constant need to be distracted.

• Thinking that the whole world is against us.

• Incapable of taking any risks.

• Feeling unlucky.

• Tendency to always be thinking of the future.

• Constant need for approval.

• Seeing the glass as always half empty.

• Irrational fear of what could happen.

• Lack of personal projects.

- Intent of finding purpose through other people's lives.

- Avoid responsibility over own actions.

- Feelings of superiority.

- Inferiority complex.

- Incapable of living in the present.

- Desire to have power.

- Obsession for success.

If you have read carefully and in a humble manner, you will probably reach the same conclusion as me:

WE ALL FUNCTION POORLY

A lapidary phrase for a manual of this type.

If you have reached this point, it means that you are like me, and like millions of other people. You are looking for something.

If everybody or almost all the products work badly, maybe this means the product -the human being- is not as perfect as I portrayed before.

THAT IS NOT CORRECT.

…Or maybe it is just that getting this product to achieve its goal of happiness is very hard.

Again, I do not think so.

Here, you, the User, can think that I am either enlightened or a trickster.

The truth is you can think whatever you want. I consider myself a seeker; I look for answers and I am sharing those that work for me. Allow me, once again, to tell you about a story I read once, which I found very funny.

One very dark night, there was a man, on his hands and knees in front of a fire. He was going backwards, forwards and in circles around the fire, as if he was looking for something.

A person walking by stopped and stared at him.

— Have you lost something? — he asked, trying to help.

— The keys of my house! — he answered, without stopping his search.

The other man knelt and started to search for them, too. But there were no keys, and he needed to continue on his way. He did not wish to appear rude, so he asked:

— Are those keys important?

— Of course! If I do not find them, I cannot get inside my house —answered the other man, shaking off the dirt from his clothes.

— And are you completely sure that you lost them here? — the man insisted.

— No, I lost them in the forest...

— And why are you looking for them here, then?

— Because it is dark in there, and here there is light.

Sometimes, the secret is knowing where to search; other times, we need to turn the house upside down until we find what we lost.

Just like you, I did not know where to look, and I never had an instruction manual. That is why I thought that if I knew how we work, I could learn to find —and fix— the failures of this product we call *human being*.

IT'S POSSIBLE THAT MY KEY DOESN'T WORK FOR YOU, AND YOURS IS SOMEWHERE ELSE...

IF THAT 'S THE CASE, DON'T STOP LOOKING!

NORMAL FUNCTIONING

It might seem obvious that the correct or normal functioning of the human being as a product is just the opposite of how it has been presented in the previous part. But to be more specific, I would like to make a list of those symptoms or clues that show what correct functioning is:

THE OBJECTS AND ACCESSORIES I ACQUIRE ARE NOT A GOAL; THEY ARE JUST TOOLS THAT MAKE MY LIFE EASIER. This doesn't mean that ideally, we should be as poor as rats. One can be rich and not be a slave of what one possesses. This is not easy, because those who do not pay attention to the last model of car or their third beach house, generally do not worry if they have more or less. The only important thing is that what we have helps us to fulfil our goals and projects.

I CAN BE ALONE. Furthermore, in some moments I need my own company; I like to enjoy myself, focusing on me and loving myself. This makes me feel at home, and happy, so later on I am able to connect with others and work in networks without losing my own identity.

MY PATH IS ONLY MINE Nobody can walk it for me, and I cannot change mine for someone else's. My way is not harder, nor easier than the path that others have; it all depends on how hard I make my path for myself. This path of life is like any other, it has signs, rocks, crossroads and junctions, walls and shortcuts.

I AM AWARE AND ALERT This does not mean that I should always be focused, or that I may not get distracted, but when I walk, I cannot have my eyes closed, because I will not see the signs. Also, I cannot have my Mind on autopilot, because I will lose all references.

NOBODY IS AGAINST ME, BUT IT'S INEVITABLE THAT I WILL BUMP INTO OTHERS, OR TO INTRUDE ON THEIR PATH, MAKING THEM THINK I WANT TO TAKE SOMETHING FROM THEM. It is normal for someone who puts all of his or her energy into having money to attack a person who wants to take some of it. Does that mean we should let others step on me? No, but one thing is defending yourself, and another thing is to react aggressively.

LIFE IS A RISK, LIKE ANY OTHER UNKNOWN PATH. I will not jump from a cliff and think that nothing will happen to me. But I will not sit on the side of the road to avoid the risk of walking.

THE FORTUNE OR LACK OF IT ARE SUBJECTIVE. I cannot avoid feeling pain or suffering. The only thing I can do is to wait for it to pass, and then take the situation as an experience. It could have been a very bad experience, but it will always help us to understand something better than we did before. I will not try to analyse the situation while I am still hurting and in pain.

THE FUTURE IS THE ONLY SITUATION THAT NEVER ARRIVES, BECAUSE WHEN IT DOES IT'S THE PRESENT. I can foresee, organize, I can plan or even dream *now*, but I cannot live in a place that does not exist.

THE PAST IS GONE. From it only experience is left. While I walk it's inevitable I look back, it gives me a sense of where I am, and strength to continue on my way. But chewing over the past like a ball of hair will only steal all my energy and paralyse me.

IT'S IMPOSSIBLE TO PLEASE EVERYONE. The important thing for me is that I did as well as I could. There will always be people who will admire us, and people who will criticize us. I can say thanks to those who admire me, because I did it right. I can also say thank you to those who criticize me, because probably I could have done it better. But neither of those opinions will ever affect my self-esteem because only I know that I really did the best I could.

THE BEST IS YET TO COME. Maybe today my situation is not the best, but can I do anything else right now?

NOBODY IS WITHOUT FEAR OF THE UNKNOWN. Fear is a mechanism from the Mind that keeps me aware of possible danger and that helps me analyse different situations carefully. Fear is good; but it is not ok to let my fear stops me. I would rather fall because I have been walking, than stay still from fear of falling.

WE ALL HAVE OUR PERSONAL PROJECT. AND IT IS ONLY OURS. The paths other people have may appear tempting, but they are not mine. How do I know what my project is if I have walked many different paths while I searched for mine?

In general, the Mind understands the project our Soul needs to work on when we are eight to thirteen years old. This is, from the time we start using our reasoning until right before we start the adolescence. The only thing we need to do is to go back there.

MY LIFE IS ONLY MINE, AND IT IS UP TO ME TO DECIDE HOW TO LIVE IT. I can help my partner, my children, my friends... but their triumphs belong only to them. I can be happy for them, and even be proud of them, but their life is not my life.

I AM RESPONSIBLE OF *EVERYTHING* THAT HAPPENS TO ME. I cannot blame anybody else; my mistakes and decisions are mine. In the same way, I cannot attribute my achievements and triumphs to anyone but myself. Each mistake is an experience for me to keep; each achievement, a trampoline.

MAYBE SOME TASKS ARE EASY FOR ME. But there will be other people who are great at things I am terrible at. That is what makes me equal to everybody.

I AM NOT LESS THAN ANYBODY. I can deal with the King or the Pope, or with a beggar, and I should do so with the same respect, politeness, consideration, and empathy.

I CANNOT STOP MY THOUGHTS, BUT I CAN SLOW THEM DOWN. I cannot stop my Mind from travelling to the future or going back to the past. What I can do is to keep it busy in the present. To do so, I need it to understand that it is not my boss, but rather a secretary that should organize, plan and establish the resources I need to achieve my objectives.

IF HAVING POWER COMES WITH OTHERS' SUBMISSION, I DO NOT WANT IT. If I have to leave my project in order to achieve power, I refuse to have it. If I must manipulate, lie or use others to get power, I am not interested on having it. If my happiness comes at the price of another person's joy, it is not a real happiness.

SUCCESS IS A CONSEQUENCE, NOT A CAUSE. Success depends on my personal perception of it. If I decide to start a task, and I fight and conquer my fears, putting dedication, effort and will into what I do, I will succeed.

It does not matter if I come first, second or last; I have reached my objective, which was finishing the task I started.

THE MIND HAS A HUGE CAPABILITY TO IDEALIZE. When I start a project, I should always keep that on mind. The real results I will get are often smaller than those I imagined.

Therefore, when I am building something, I should start at the bottom, and brick by brick build my way to the roof. An alternative to this approach would be to use the same trick as when a riffle's fore sight is broken: to aim two centimetres up, and one to the left, and to hope to reach the aim.

If you, User, felt that you identified with some or all of the symptoms of abnormal functioning and think that the above symptoms of correct functioning are just a list of unrealistic wishes, keep reading. The section coming up will be of great use to you.

The Happiness.
User's manual for humans

RESETTING

By resetting, I mean the process we use to restart a product. The reason to do so is not that a product is working terribly. It could be that there are small failures that make our work slower, or maybe the case is so extreme that we cannot even control the product any more.

And you could ask me: — How do we do that?

WE GIVE UP

— What?

Yes, this is a hard task, because the Mind does not give up easily. And it's normal, because it can look back to the past and forward to the future, imagining whatever it wants. But these imaginings are not real.

The only thing that is real is what happens today. If today you find yourself stumbling upon the exact same rock for the thousandth time, it means that you should stop running in circles.

Give up. It is obvious that something does not work. You want to be happy, and your Soul wants you to be happy, but the Mind has taken control over the situation and it is unable to find the key to achieve such an objective.

The Mind fantasizes about how everything will be great someday, and when nothing changes, it moves back to the past, looking for someone to blame.

— If I had done this differently...

— If I had made a different decision...

Wake up! You cannot go back! In the past, you did the best you could with what you had, and you made your decisions based on what you thought was best.

Stop, Mind, just stop! We know that this path leads us to nowhere. I am thankful for your work, but let the Soul take control.

I am going to give an example of this.

A few years back, I was in a very hard financial situation. I worked hard and put a lot of effort into my work, but was only barely surviving. To top it all my car, which was my life line to work, broke down. I had no money to fix it and less to buy another one. My Mind was constantly thinking of the things I wanted to do, but that did not change anything. I felt that everything was a disaster. I lived in a very small town and a car was indispensable to carry out a normal life. Not being able to drive around was a real tragedy.

I remember walking down the street with a huge sense of unease.

I had analysed all my options: I could ask for a bank loan, but I rejected the idea because I already had a debt and it was hard enough as it was to pay it back. I could play the lottery, but I needed the money I had and I couldn't risk it that way. Suddenly, I felt a creak inside of me, as if something inside me had broken. This was followed by a feeling of abandonment and peace.

I heard a voice inside of me saying:

—It is nobody's fault, you have done the best you could... the solution will present itself.

My Mind was still agitated, and at times, it would analyse again all the possible solutions, just to go back to a calm state few seconds later.

—There is no solution —, my Mind murmured, defeatedly. The rest of me wasn't nervous or uneasy. I even felt happy because I could do stuff I had wanted to do for a long time: I could take a walk on the beach, exercise, organize my papers, and I could write more...

Two days later, a friend called me and offered me his second car. I could borrow it as he did not need it. Among the papers I organized, I found an insurance claim I didn't know about... and just like that, I had a car to go to work, money to buy another second hand one, and I even got a great price for it.

I could tell you many stories like this, but still, the Mind always tends to do its thing: it wants to solve everything, and to control everything. I do believe that it takes its job too seriously, assuming responsibilities that are not for the mind.

But the Mind forgets that it is just a secretary! It should analyse situations, and provide the Soul with possible options. But it is not the one in charge of making decisions; the Soul is. The Soul has:

THE STRENGTH NEEDED TO CHANGE WHAT CAN BE CHANGED, TO ACCEPT THAT WHICH CAN'T BE CHANGED, AND THE WISDOM TO KNOW THE DIFFERENCE.

Yes, I know. The expression is not mine. It belongs to the Serenity prayer, attributed to theologian and writer Reinhold Niebuhr.

"Father, give us courage to change what must be altered, serenity to accept what cannot be helped, and the insight to know the one from the other."

That is the most popular part, but the prayer continues:

"Living one day at a time,
Enjoying one moment at a time,
Accepting hardship as a pathway to peace,
Taking, as Jesus did,
This sinful world as it is,
Not as I would have it,
Trusting that You will make all things right,
If I surrender to Your will,
So that I may be reasonably happy in this life,
And supremely happy with You forever in the next.
Amen."

It is not bad, but my humble opinion is that the author put all expectations on someone else, not on himself.

We really do not need to ask anybody for anything; strength is not given, it comes from inside.

I would like to point out User, that I have never used the word resignation. I find it a terrible term that reminds me of something said at a funeral parlour:

"Resignation… we are nothing"

What a shitty phrase!

What do they mean by saying "we are nothing"?We are a miracle from the Universe!

To give up, and accept situations for what they are has nothing to do with resignation.

As I've mentioned death, I would like to add a reflection.

The reality is that our body and our Mind will die. That is the ultimate resetting of our system. And it surprises me that despite death being the most real fact of our existence, we avoid talking about it. We don't study this subject at school, and we are definitely never ready for it when it arrives.

There is drink advert I really like. It is on TV, and it says that the only capital we have is time, and that it's up to us how we spend it. The creator behind that idea is a genius. Have you ever thought about it in that way?

The crucial point is that we do not really know how much time we actually have, and because of that we shouldn't waste it on trivialities. Therefore, if your operative system is working badly, focus on one problem you cannot solve and then give up on it. Focus on the *now* and not on the problem, and tell your Mind to let it go.

"If a problem has a solution, there's no need to worry about it. If a problem does not have a solution, worrying won't find one."

Giving up doesn't mean being apathetic or putting your Mind on autopilot. The Mind should at all times be aware of possible signs along the way. We never know where the solution will come from! But at the same time, it should be focused on the present, planning what to do today, in ten minutes, or in one hour.

Is this too much work?

I don't think so! The Mind is an efficient secretary it can do that and much more. Do not forget that at your disposal you have a central computer with 2,5 *petabytes* of storage and millions of active neurones. But to use it properly, you need to remember that your real "You" is located in your Soul, not in your Mind.

What about my projects and dreams? Should I forget about them?

Not at all.

Until not so long ago the screensaver on my computer said:

«IT'S NOT WRONG TO BUILD CASTLES IN THE AIR; BUT YOU SHOULD START WITH FOUNDATIONS»

One can order the Mind to plan a project, and it will do it thoroughly. But once the planning ends, the Mind cannot just stay there, hanging on the future. It is useless to just dream, because the foundations of the dreams and the projects need to be laid today.

Do you remember the tale of those two kids who dreamt of being famous tennis players?

BE CAREFUL: DAY DREAMING CAN BE ADDICTIVE!

But, what happens if I cannot lay the foundations of my project right now?

Just keep doing what you are doing. Do not think about it anymore. Enjoy what you are doing now! Put all your attention and energy into it. Even the most boring tasks can teach us something.

Here's another true story.

When I was ten years old, my mum signed me up to take English classes at the Rosarine Association of English Culture. The beginner's classes took place in cramped rooms in a very old building.

The teacher only spoke in English; she was old, small, and strict.

After some time, I realised that she was actually a wonderful person, but in the beginning I was just afraid of her. The discipline at that school was rigorous; they demanded English style punctuality, and the security guard looked like she came from a juvenile detention center. That wasn't all, the whole first year consisted of learning a phonetic system. We did not really learn English. We would just repeat sounds, like parrots.

To have to endure this for an hour, three times a week, would make anyone's wish to learn a language, diminish. But my mum didn't want me to stop. After the first year, I got the taste for it. Either that, or I was just enjoying getting out of the house. The point is, I graduated with high grades and made great friends along the way.

But, what did I need English for? We lived in an immigrant's neighbourhood, with most of our neighbours being Italian, Spanish or Russian, but no English. At home, nobody spoke English and the chances of me using it in the future were small.

When I was thirteen my relationship with my parents and the whole world was turned upside down. I had no real role models, nobody to talk to, and I felt trapped and hopeless.

I distracted myself by reading, studying, and playing sports, but I always had to go back home, where I was unhappy. I had bad dreams every night.

One summer night, I decided that I'd had enough, and that I needed to relax. Without really knowing what I was doing I started breathing deeply, holding my breath for some seconds, and then letting it go slowly. This gave me feeling of peace, and I could see a blue dot in front of me through my closed eyes. I dreamt that I was boarding a plane: I could see myself waving goodbye on the stairs, and I could hear the engines starting up. I landed in Europe, and more specifically, in London. I don't remember all the details of that dream; but I do recall feeling free and happy the next morning. However, life was the same, maybe worse as my chances of travel were zero. For many nights, I tried to have the same dream, practising my breath exercises, but in vain.

Time went by, and I would sometimes think of those feelings of freedom and joy, but I never dreamt again about that trip. I focused on what I was supposed to do: studying, and attending two catholic groups for young people.

When I was in my last year of secondary school, the headmaster called the three best students from the final and penultimate years of the school. One of them was me.

He explained to us that the Argentinian Airlines was organizing a quiz competition, and the prize... was a trip to Europe! My dream came back to me, clearer than ever before.

The competition was on TV, they simulated a journey and for each step there was a question. Whoever answered the eight questions would win a plane ticket to the corresponding destination.

Two of us signed up: myself and a student from the course below me. When we arrived at the TV studio, they explained how the system worked. There were twenty-two schools signed up and participation was decided through a raffle. The first participant to answer all the questions correctly won and the rest were out of the competition. The rest of potential participants were supposed to go to the studio every Monday, in case the participant failed a question. If you could not show up, you were disqualified.

The general reaction was one of having been deceived. It was easier to win the lottery than having a chance in that competition. Some indignantly pulled out, and in the end, there were only thirteen schools competing.

When we took the raffle number that determined our turn to participate, we got thirteen. We were last! This meant that, for us to even have a chance to participate, everybody else had to fail.

The other student gave up, but I accepted. I kept going to the TV studio every Monday for the next three months. I needed to take two buses to get there from home, and then more public transportation to get to school. Overall, I think I probably travelled the same distance that exists between Europe and Argentina in those months.

Time passed, and students would give right answers, and wrong ones. When the penultimate program arrived, the student who was competing was right in all questions, except the last one. Finally, it was my turn.

The director of the program decided that it was obvious that eight questions was too much for us to answer at once, so they reduced the number to six. They decided that if I was unable to win, they could send the money of the ticket to some Non-profit organization; punctually to a catholic Orphan's hospice. This left the priest of the school rubbing his hands.

When Monday came, half my school came along to give me moral support. I was not aware of the expectation this competition had roused. I found out later that it was one of the largest audiences in the history of the program.

I answered four questions, all correctly, but I was starting to feel nervous. On the fifth question, I had doubts about the answer, and time was running out. Despite this, I answered it correctly.

The sixth question was asked after the last pause for commercials. The program was about to end. When they put it to me, I could not help smiling. I had read the answer that same morning...

So then, at seventeen years old, and four years after that strange dream I'd had, I travelled to London. The effort of learning English made sense. It was the best trip of my life; it made me grow up quickly and it certainly changed my point of view on life. I also learnt a lot about tv, which helped me in the coming years. I overcame my stage fright, learnt that everything happens for a reason, and that I should never give up on my dreams. The Universe has its own pace, and everything arrives when it should, but not necessarily when we want it to.

Maybe you don't believe such a story. It's the first time I have put it down on paper and as I was writing it seemed quite miraculous even to me. I must say that I avoided adding many more interesting details to keep it as short as possible.

WHEN YOU HAVE AN OVERWHELMING PROBLEM OR A DREAM THAT SEEMS IMPOSSIBLE, DO THE BEST YOU CAN. IF YOU CAN'T FIND A SOLUTION, LEAVE IT. RESET YOUR SYSTEM AND CARRY ON DOING THE BEST YOU CAN, TODAY.

GUARANTEE

Now you, User, could think that such a sophisticated system as the human being must have a great guarantee.

NOT REALLY.

The product *human being* has no guarantee. It is true that we make thousands of new ones everyday, and we have advanced a lot regarding our reproduction. But the manufacturer who invented and patented this product is unknown. Therefore, there is no one to send our complaints to.

And you might say:

—Just put a man and a woman together and watch how they make them.

In reality two halves of a series of chromosomes are combined and grow into a new product. This has also been done in a laboratory and it has been taken even further with the creation of an artificial cell. Quite possibly, with investigation and effort we may be able to make an artificial human being in some years. Just like the one we have described in this manual. But what about the Soul? We'll see about that when the time comes.

If you are religious, you will probably tell me that God, Jehovah or in whatever name you were baptised is the real manufacturer. As far as I know, they all guarantee eternal life and complete happiness after death.

In that case, the guarantee is effective the moment this product called human being ceases to live together with all its components. Which, in other words, means that on this planet such a guarantee does not exist.

Obviously, I do not intend to offend anybody. If you are feeling annoyed right now, you can stop reading now. But if you decide to continue, let me repeat that everything I am telling you is a result of my own experience. As I said in the beginning, I am not here to re-invent the wheel neither am I a scientist or an atheist.

To understand the guarantee offered to the faithful from the church I would like to differentiate between Church and Religion.

The word Church comes from the latin *ecclesia* and greek ἐκκληοία, transcribed as *ekklēsía*, it means nothing more than a congregation of citizens dealing with important issues, generally regarding politics. In the sacred writings, the word *ecclesia* refers to the congregation of the people of Israel, specifically.

The word religion, on the other hand, comes from the term *religar*, *religare* o *re-legere* in latin, which means to unite two elements that had been separated previously. The idea comes from the Genesis book, in which Adam and Eve are expelled from Paradise because they ate the fruit of the forbidden tree. The consequences are all the tragedies that human beings suffer: painful birth, death, sickness, and the lack of knowledge about who we are and where we are going.

LET US SAY THAT IT SEEMS LIKE A TALE IN WHICH THE NAUGHTY KID IS PUNISHED BY HIS DAD BECAUSE HE DID SOMETHING WRONG.

Maybe that worked in the times of the ancient Hebrews, but what about now? And that's without mentioning that this story is probably the start of the machismo that has devastated the Occidental world for the last two thousand years. From the book of Genesis, we can read:

Now the serpent was more subtle than any beast of the field which LORD God had made. He said to the woman, " Has God not said that "You must not eat from any tree in the garden'?" The woman said to the serpent, "We may eat fruit from the trees in the garden, but God did say, 'You must not eat fruit from the tree that is in the middle of the garden, and you must not touch it, or you will die.'" "You will surely not die," the serpent said to the woman."For God knows that when you eat from it your eyes will be opened, and you will be like God, knowing good and evil." When the woman saw that the fruit of the tree was good for food and pleasing to the eye, and also desirable for gaining wisdom, she took some and ate it. She also gave some to her husband, who was with her, and he ate it. Then the eyes of both of them were opened, and they realized they were naked; so, they sewed fig leaves together and made coverings for themselves.

Then the man and his wife heard the sound of the LORD God as he was walking in the garden in the cool of the day, and they hid from the LORD God among the trees of the garden.

We all know how this story continues: God punishes Adam for listening to Eve, so in other words, she is to blame for dragging the man to sin.

What a child's story!

To top it all, this tale is not even original; the Hebrews took it from previous traditions, possibly the Sumerians from the mesopotamian valley.

Have you ever played Chinese whispers?

It was very popular when I was a child, and it goes like this: the first player whispers a phrase in someone's ear, and they repeat the phrase to someone else, and so on. When the last player hears the phrase, it sounds very different than the original one. The same happens with the oral traditions; maybe the main message is kept, but the details are changed and distorted generation after generation.

Some day I will tell you the origin of this silly idea of the woman being inferior to the man. Or you could look it up yourself.

IT IS TRULY PATHETIC!

Now, let us get back to religion and the Church.

The Anthropologist Clifford Geertz[12] defined religion in the following manner:

---

[12]Clifford Geertz (1926 -2006). American anthropologist. He studied at Antioch College, where he graduated in 1950; Graduated from Harvard as a Ph.D. in 1956. Part of the team of anthropologists at the University of Chicago was later professor of social sciences at the Institute for Advanced Study 1970-2000. He received an honorary doctorate from Bates College in 1980.

"Religion is a system of symbols which acts to establish powerful, pervasive and long-lasting moods and motivations... Moods are the way we respond to and feel about the world. Motives are the things we aspire to; the values we hold. These two together make up our way of life or ethos. Religious symbols therefore tell us that, because reality is constructed in a certain way, we ought to feel a certain way and aim to fulfill certain values. They also tell us that, because reality is constructed in a particular way, those particular feelings are especially rewarding and those values can, in fact, be fulfilled."

Do you remember the mirror neurones?

The same effect caused by either a football team or your favourite singer. And the Church is not so different; it also has fans and supporters. The energy that they emit is exactly the same because the mirror neurones do not tell apart the sacred from the profane, the good from the bad. They just search for other neurones to empathize with.

Maybe the biggest difference between football fans and a church is that the religious churches have a big element of control among their believers: fear of the unknown. Maybe for that reason, the church and the power have always been allies.

I must say, football has more and more fanaticism around it. Maybe because people believe a little less in churches...

At this point, you could argue:

—But I am just following the sacred Scriptures, or the Gospels!

In that case, let me tell you that the Gospels were written on paper almost a century after Christ had died in the Cross. His apostles had died, too. So, more or less, the Church council met and decided what to accept and what to reject from the story that some Christians had written about what others said about Messiah's words.

Does that mean that all we have learned from religion is a lie?

No!

I just mean that it is a biased truth, a manipulated story. In any case, whatever you decide to believe depends on your faith. In my case, I do not believe that in order to be happy, we need to obey specific rules or follow commandments and even less, that we need to be miserable in this life to be happy in the next one. That just sounds like domination and manipulation.

When I say that it's all a matter of faith whether you believe or not in the churches, I mean that the product human being has a very valuable attribute, called *freedom*. We will talk about it in the next section.

Now, let us go back to the topic of the guarantee.

THE ONLY GUARANTEE OF REACHING THE GOAL IS BY THE PRODUCT ITSELF. THE ONLY ONE RESPONSIBLE FOR THIS IS YOU, DEAR USER.

The only one responsible for being happy is yourself, User. And not in a future life that might not even exist, but in this one. The model you have acquired has all the components it needs to achieve such happiness. And if you think you cannot do it, you can always use the reset function to start again.

USE YOUR GUARANTEE!

FREEDOM

What a word! It is almost as happiness, and like it, many authors have tried to define it in some way. It seems as freedom and happiness go well together.

I will start by saying that freedom is an attribute, a quality that the human being has. Therefore, it is something we have and we should never fear losing it. However, how many of us feel sometimes, trapped?

I would say everybody feels that way sometimes.

We live in a society full of limitations, in which you can't just do whatever you please. Often, you do what others expect you to do.

ISN'T THAT SLAVERY?

Yes.

IS IT SOCIETY'S FAULT?

No.

In reality, people can do as they please, but they cannot avoid the consequences that their actions bring.

I can rob a bank. And they deserve to be robbed, because they are often thieves, liars and scammers themselves. So, who is stopping me? Nobody, really.

So why don't I do it?

Oh! What if they catch me? What if they kill me? What if I go to jail?

Therefore, I don't do it because of the possible consequences, for fear of the reprisals.

What I mean is that the phrase 'we are free' is valid, it's an attribute of the product human being. We can use our freedom whenever we want, but we can't avoid the consequences of our actions.

Years ago, I wrote a novel about a historical event in which lack of freedom was the main topic. I am talking about what happened during the Spanish Civil War and the Second World War. The events were told to me by a lovely lady who died while I was still writing her story. In the phase of investigation, which preceded the writing of the book, I heard several testimonies from survivors from Mauthausen and Gusen concentration camps. Something caught my attention: in the camps, it was a handful of german soldiers who kept locked more than 40,000 prisoners, using them as forced labour and starving them to death. I never found reference of any riots. Why?

FEAR...

As I said previously, fear is a built-in safety mechanism of the *human being* and is located in the Mind. The Mind sends an alert when it is faced with a potentially dangerous or unknown situation, and gets the body ready to either attack or escape.

The symptoms of fear are clear:

- **Increase heartbeat.**
- **Tense muscles**
- **Stomach contraction**
- **Emptying of the intestines**
- **Release of adrenaline and noradrenaline**
- **Increase of feelings of alarm**

So far, so good. But the problem is that the Mind can only perceive a small part of reality, so it interprets the stimuli the senses send it and fills the gaps with past experiences. Therefore, if a dog bit you when you were young, just seeing one sets your Mind on alert. Until when you walk home on a dark, lonely street, you may think you see dogs waiting in every corner. This irrational fear in situations that are really not dangerous can undermine your freedom to go out for a walk in the dark, or even quash your decision to have a pet.

WHY DOES THIS HAPPEN?

This happens because your consciousness lives in the Mind, not in the Soul. The Mind is in charge, and as I said on many occasions, the position of Manager is too much for it, it's good at being a secretary.

Does that mean that if the consciousness was located in the Soul we would feel no fear?

We would feel fear anyway, as it is a protective mechanism, an automatic reaction. But we'd be able to face it.

This a simple, personal example:

Rats are small animals, just like any other. They have lively eyes and a likeable face, and they are very clever.

They live in organized colonies, take care of their babies and they never attack other animals or human beings unless they feel threatened. However, they are often hated, feared and vilified. With the exception of Mickey Mouse who nobody remembers when one of these rodents gets in their house.

When I was a child, I lived in a house that was surrounded by empty plots. And obviously, there were rats. My mother was so scared of them that when she saw one, she would hop on a table or chair and scream as if possessed. My grandmother had told me that rats carry many sicknesses around, like bubonic plague, which -according to her- had killed one of my relatives while she was pregnant. She also told me that rats often bite children while they sleep.

Obviously, all those stories changed my perception. One day, my mother asked me to take out the rubbish and when I lifted the lid of the bin, I found myself face to face with a rat. The poor little animal looked at me curiously, but my Mind unleashed the danger alert and I felt an inexplicable panic. I remember that I started trembling and I couldn't speak. For the rest of the day, I stood on guard in front of that door, without daring to open it again. In the evening, the effects of my panic had dissolved, but not completely.

I remembered that I had seen rats before; one of my friends had hamsters and I thought they were cute. So, I decided to open the door and tell the little animal that it should go away because I needed to take the rubbish out. But as I got closer to the door, I panicked again and started trembling. Despite this I forced myself to carry out my task. I opened the door, but I could not see anything. I felt relieved and I even thought that I had telepathically removed them. I picked up the rubbish, and suddenly I saw in a corner not one but two rats. That was unbearable, my fear was taking over and that was a feeling I did not like at all.

I had been this afraid before, of the dark, and then my sister couldn't sleep with the light off. Even though I was trembling, I armed myself with a broom and asked my mum to boil a pan of water. When the water was ready, I took the saucepan, I opened the shed and I threw the water inside. One of the rats died instantly, and I followed the other one and killed it with the broom. My teeth were chattering and I had to run to the toilet. However, I felt happy and euphoric, because I had faced my fear.

Since that day, I've killed a lot of rats, by doing that I have learnt that yes I feel fear, but it doesn't paralyse me anymore.

I feel sad for the rats I have killed, because after all, they have as much right to live as I do, but I do not like them running around inside my house. I often see rats in the mountain, and it gives me shivers, but that's all. They are in their habitat and it doesn't bother me.

Am I a hero?

No. I still feel fear. The only difference is that now I know I can face it and conquer it.

AND THEREIN LIES FREEDOM.

With any other situation, the solution is the same, even fear of leaving our comfort zone.

There is another reaction in the face of fear: sometimes, we become addicted to the adrenaline rush. This happens among those who practice extreme sports or who ride on roller-coasters. After the fear passes, the Mind feels relaxed and assumes that it is necessary to put oneself in danger in order to feel great. Again, it is the Mind -not the Soul- who follows this logic. The wish to feel the adrenaline makes some take unnecessary risks, and often the results are fateful.

The correct mechanism when the Soul is in charge is as it follows:

1. My soul decides to do something because it thinks it's part of my path to happiness.

2. My mind exposes the dangers and releases the fear alert. The point is not to feel the adrenaline rush, but to do something the Mind considers potentially dangerous, such as leaving the comfort zone.

3. The Essence decides there is no option, and despite the fear, orders to continue.

4. The mind and the body put all sensors on alert, adrenaline is released but I can face any danger with total control over my faculties.

This is useful for a job interview, to move from one country to another, to get a divorce or to move to a new house. It is the freedom to decide we want to take a risk to achieve a higher goal. We are always able to use this freedom when the Soul is behind the decision.

Fear is the main element the powerful have used to restrict people's freedom. The more thoughtless the population is, the more fear they have and the bigger the need for those in charge to set rules and establish limits. Leaving that situation comes with the loss of security and comes with the responsibility to decide for oneself, which produces fear. Using fear as a tool has been so successful that those in power have transformed the whole world into a global concentration camp.

They decide, and you obey. The sophistication of the system is such that you think that you are deciding for yourself. But there is something we can't get around: we do feel frightened and trapped without solution. Those two elements accumulated produce a sickness never seen before, called Negative Stress. The continuous presence of small or large pressures on the Mind results in a continuous perception of dangers, to which it needs to react.

You must obey because, if not...

You might lose all your money, and you would not be able to feed your family. You would become an offender, people would speak badly of you, you would not be able to fulfill your obligations, you would fall out of favour, go to jail, and become a social outcast. In the US, they have a term for it: loser. A loser is someone who is outside the system.

What about those who are inside?

It's enough to watch any American movie to understand the levels of stress and the ridiculous demands that are placed on workers in order for them to have a dignified standard of living.

I am now going to tell you a story.

On a little-known Spanish ranch, two goat kids were born at the same time, from different mothers. There were called Coal and Moon.

Coal was born in the farmyard, which was separated from the open forest by an electric wire. Moon was born in the middle of the forest, wild.

One day, the two little goats met face to face, with only the electric wire separating them.

– Come play with me! – invited Moon – We have the whole forest to run, jump and have fun in.

– My mum says I cannot – answered Coal – she says that I am a farm goat and that I should learn to behave as one. Plus, these wires are electrified and I cannot jump without touching them.

– Alright, it is your choice – said Moon, and she ran into the forest. She spent hours and hours investigating the caves, running after the birds, chasing squirrels and eating any green grass she found in her way.

Coal on the other hand received his feed, drank his mother's milk and trotted around the farm quietly. He needed to be a well-behaved goat even though inside he felt the need to run and jump.

The next day, Moon came back.

– Are you sure that you do not want to come play with me? Yesterday I found a beautiful cave and there are some funny flowers that make you sneeze when you eat them!

– I cannot, today I have to learn the farmer's language, who is the one who feeds us.

Moon went back to the forest, running and jumping, and feeling sorry for Coal. When she was about to eat a very appealing sprout of fennel, she noticed a very strange, alarming smell on the wind. All of her body tensed and she regretted being so far from her mother at that moment. For a minute, she was frozen to the spot. But the smell was becoming more and more intense, and something in her brain made her run as fast as she could. Moon ran and jumped all the way back home without looking back, as if someone was following her. She only stopped when she ran out of strength and the strong musk smell had disappeared all together.

"Maybe Coal is lucky, after all", she thought as she tried to catch her breath "In the forest there are beautiful things, but also lots of danger... Like the wolves, for example. Or you can fall and break a leg, and then the birds of pray will come and finish you off... Or you could eat a poisonous plant by mistake and nobody would call the vet... And if the Spring is very dry, it is hard to find food. But he has a food ration everyday, no matter what..."

Moon spent a few days thinking about this, walking around without enthusiasm and or appetite. Finally, she decided to go back and talk to Coal. Maybe this time he would want to play with her in the forest, and they could face any coming danger together. Or maybe she would decide to stay in the farm and learn to be a farm goat.

As she approached the farm, she started feeling mistrust and discouraged. By the time she reached the wires, Moon there was an ugly smell in her nose. Coal was hanging from a hook next to the other goats of his age, and the farmer had started skinning them...

FREEDOM IS DANGEROUS BUT DOMESTICATION IS FATAL.

Freedom is an attribute that *human beings* are manufactured with, and to use that freedom is the only way to reach the goal of happiness.

What would it happen if everybody agreed not to buy a specific product?

The company producing it would either put the price down or go under.

I can give you an example:

Around 1800, the tea importers put up the price of tea in England. The tea consumers decided not to buy it even though it was their favourite drink. The warehouses started to fill up, the tea went bad and they had to throw tons of it into the Thames river. As a consequence, the price went down and nobody thought of putting it up again.

What would happen if people decided not to work for any companies who don't treat their employees with respect?

What if people stopped paying taxes when they became excessive?

Of course, it is not that easy even though we see in the social media that we have the power to make free decisions when we unite. In the everyday life, this is more complicated. If you don't believe me, try to start complaining and demanding your rights in a public space. The first reaction you will get from other people is to look to the away. The fear to question the established order is such that not even the mirror neurones work in some situations.

For that reason, User, if you want to be happy practice your freedom. Use it. As any other skill, if you do not use it, it rusts.

And at this point, you probably think that the theory is very easy, and that things get more complicated with a mortgage and kids to support...

For sure you have a point. You won't become in the next Che Guevara in one day. And that is not even advisable, considering how that idealist ended up.

However, you can use your freedom in small doses, like training to become better at using it. Think of a situation that annoys you, then the possible actions to resolve the situation.

Then analyse the possible consequences of your actions, and think if you really want to act on it, and consider if you will feel better or worse afterwards. And then, just do it!

Maybe this sounds silly, but perhaps, the simple fact of leaving our comfort zone is enough for us to feel freer and happier.

Here is an example:

One of the many things I've done in my life was starting a business from zero, without having much to invest. I did it during a huge economic crisis and I started step by step in order to avoid failure. I thought that by offering a good and pleasing customer service, and being very careful with my investments, everything was going to be ok. Everybody knows that in sales, success depends on the empathy between seller and customer. That is, if our mirror neurones make contact and get along with the ones in our client's brains, we are halfway there.

I must say I am very good at doing that, but after three years, I felt stuck and frustrated. The clients got used to me always doing what they wanted, and started to take my diligence for granted. They could pay me however they chose. After all, a small amount of money made the difference between being able to put gas in my car or not.

The situation was annoying for me, because I was offering my best and my clients were taking advantage of it. I thought of all the options I had to turn the situation around. They all involved a greater effort on my part, and taking risks that I was not ready to take. In the end, I saw that I was between a rock and a hard place and had no choice but to continue as I was, or to put sale conditions that I thought were fair. I was sure that, by deciding the latter, I would lose sales and clients, and maybe that would force me to close my business. I was afraid because all my money was invested in it, and I did not have any other source of income. To top it all, I was over fifty years old, which made it harder for me to get another job. However, I decided that despite the risks, I did not want to continue doing business like that. I understood that I was staying in my comfort zone even though I was annoyed in it. One day, I woke up in the morning, and decided to tell all my clients that the conditions had changed; I would set the rules to pay, and they could not just call me anytime expecting me to run to them.

Do you know what happened?

I did not need to open my mouth. I had changed my attitude, and my clients' mirror neurones had adapted quickly to that change. I started to earn more money, and I did not lose a single client. I felt happy.

A CHANGE IN THE VIBRATION GENERATES A CHANGE IN THE MANIFESTATION

A change in the vibration creates a change in the manifestation. This is the consequence of one of the seven principles of Hermes Trismegisto[13].

Metaphysics has always been one of the sources I used in order to try to understand and solve my problems. I hope you do not think that I have ever been involved with witchcraft, but if you choose to believe that, you can.

---

[13] Hermes Trismegisto: is the purported author of the **Hermetic Corpus**, a series of sacred texts that are the basis of **Hermeticism**. Hermes Trismegistus is mentioned primarily in occult literature as the Egyptian sage, parallel to the god, also Egyptian, who created alchemy and developed a system of metaphysical beliefs that is now known as hermeticism. To some medieval thinkers, Hermes Trismegistus was a pagan prophet who announced the advent of Christianity.

The hermetic principles have been applied and explained by several esoteric and metaphysical schools, and it seems like they were a source of inspiration for many well-known scientifics and artists. Among them, we can find Isaac Newton, Leonardo da Vinci, Galileo Galilei, John Locke and Albert Einstein.

In case you are interested, here is a list of those principles. I took them from "The Kybalion"[14]

1. **MENTALISM**. All is Mind. Everything that happens is the result of the mental state which proceeds it.

2. **CORRESPONDENCE**. As above, so below; as below, so above. There is always a correspondence between the laws of phenomena of the various "planes" of being and life. This principle takes place in the Physical, the Mental and the Spiritual planes.

3. **VIBRATION**. Nothing is immobile; everything moves, everything has a vibration. A change in the vibration generates a change in the manifestation.

---

[14] The Kybalion: Document of the nineteenth century that summarizes the teachings of Hermeticism, known as the seven principles of Hermeticism. His authorship is attributed to The Three Initiates, an anonymous group of occultists.

4. **POLARITY**. Everything is double, as everything has two poles. Everything has its opposite: the opposites are identical in nature but different in degree. The extremes touch, and all truth is half true. Any paradox can be reconciled.

5. **RHYTHM**. The Principle of Rhythm embodies the idea that in everything there is manifested a measured motion, a to and from, a flow and ebb, a swing backward and forward, a pendulum-like movement. This principle explains that there is rhythm between every pair of opposites, or poles, and is closely related to the Principle of Polarity.

6. **CAUSE AND EFFECT**. The Principle of Cause and Effect explains that there is a cause for every effect, and an effect for every cause. It also states that there is no such thing as chance, that chance is merely a term indicating extant causes not recognized or perceived.

7. **GENDER**. There is gender in everything. Everything has masculine and feminine principles. The physic plane is the sexuality.

It is not the intention of this book to explain those principles. I am adding them here as extra information. But believe me, a huge percentage of self-help books have them as a starting point. Again, and going back to the topic we were discussing, why don't you take a problem that has no solution, and use the freedom you have to give it up? Do it, and you will see that the product *human being* is wonderful and comes with all the tools it needs to reach the goal of happiness.

The Happiness.
User's manual for humans

MESSAGE TO THE USERS

If you have arrived here by reading this whole manual, I would like to thank you. Why? Because, do you know anyone who has read a whole instruction manual? I don't.

And if you have, it is surely because you are looking for something. Maybe there are parts of your life that you do not understand; perhaps you have failed in the past and you wonder why, or maybe you have been through one or several situations that have made your whole world tremble...

Whatever the reason, I hope that my experience has been useful to you.

It is very possible that, while you were reading, you identified with some of the things I talked about, or that you even said to yourself "I knew it!".

Don't worry, that is completely normal. The important thing is that all of those things that you knew at a subconscious level, are now clearer, and therefore, you can apply them to your daily life.

The truth is, I could have never imagined that I would write this book. I love telling stories, but one day I realized that everything I wrote had an underlying meaning. My readers told me so, too. And my intention was not to help anyone, but rather to ease the urge of writing. For that reason, I thought that if I poured out all my feelings and thoughts and transformed them into words, I would empty myself and be free to just write plain stories. The problem is that I have felt so good writing this book that now I feel I have so much more to say. Therefore, I can't promise I will not do this again.

I want you to know that, even though I am not a psychologist, neurologist or doctor, You, the User, can count on me. Sometimes, a friendly hand, a little advice, suggestion or the mere action of getting something off your chest can give us the perspective we need to get ourselves balanced. Because, after all, we are the only ones who can make the human work to its full potential. Greetings from my mirror neurones.

RICARDO LAMPUGNANI

www.ingramcontent.com/pod-product-compliance
Lightning Source LLC
Chambersburg PA
CBHW062208280526
45788CB00001B/490